COMMAND ENGLISH

A Course in Military English

Students' Book

James Arnold and
Captain (Retired) Robert Sacco

Longman

Longman Group Limited,
Longman House, Burnt Mill, Harlow,
Essex CM20 2JE, England
and Associated Companies throughout the world

First published 1988
Second impression 1994

ISBN 0 582 94800 2

Produced by Longman Singapore Publishers (Pte) Ltd.
Printed in Singapore

CONTENTS

UNIFORM AND EQUIPMENT

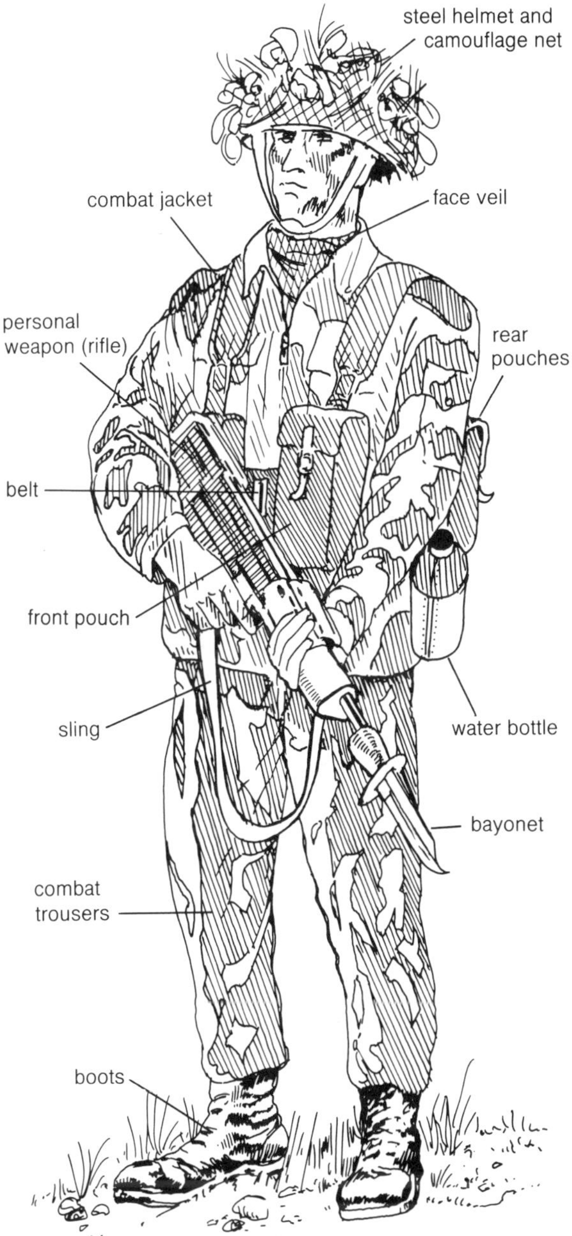

Soldier in fighting order

A PRESENTATION

Here is a soldier in a uniform called fighting order. He has a rifle as his personal weapon. There is a bayonet and a sling on the rifle.

He is in combat kit and boots. There is a camouflage net on his steel helmet and he has a face veil round his neck.

On his belt there are four pouches and a water bottle. In the two front pouches are some grenades, some ammunition for his personal weapon and also spare rounds for his section's machine gun. In his two rear pouches there are his combat rations and various items of essential personal equipment.

B COMPREHENSION

Exercise 1:1

1. Is he in civilian clothes?
2. Is his personal weapon a machine gun?
3. What is there on his rifle?
4. What is there on his steel helmet?
5. How many pouches are there on his belt?
6. Are there any grenades in his front pouches?
7. What other things are in his front pouches?
8. Are his combat rations in his rear pouches?

C GRAMMAR FOCUS

Is there a bayonet on the rifle?
Are there any magazines in the pouch?
How many magazines are there in the pouch?

Exercise 1:2

Look at the picture on the right.

Look at the model:

Question 1: Is there a sling on the rifle?
Answer 1: Yes, there is.
Question 2: Is there a bayonet on the rifle?
Answer 2: No, there isn't.

Now use these words:

weapon in his hands
steel helmet on his head
water bottle on his belt
face veil around his neck

Look at the model:
Question 3: Are there any rounds in the front pouches?
Answer 3: Yes, there are.
Question 4: Are there any maps in the front pouches?
Answer 4: No, there aren't.

Now use these words:
magazines / front pouches
combat rations / front pouches
grenades / front pouches
personal items / front pouches

Look at the model:
Question 5: How many magazines are there in the pouch?
Answer 5: There are four.

Now use these words:
rounds / in each magazine
grenades / in the pouch
spare rounds / for the machine gun

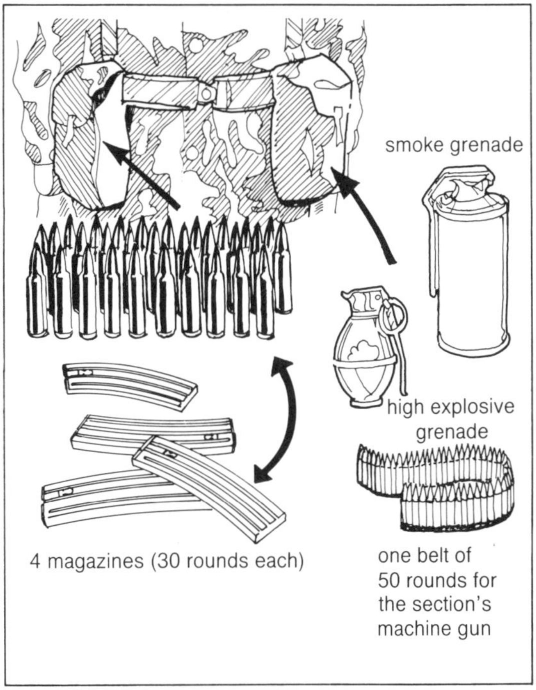

Contents of front pouches

There is/are some There isn't/aren't any How many ....?

Exercise 1:3
Make sentences from the tables.

Countable nouns

There are	four three ten two six	bottles. notices. rounds. jackets. items of equipment.

Uncountable nouns

There is	some	water. information. ammunition. clothing. equipment.

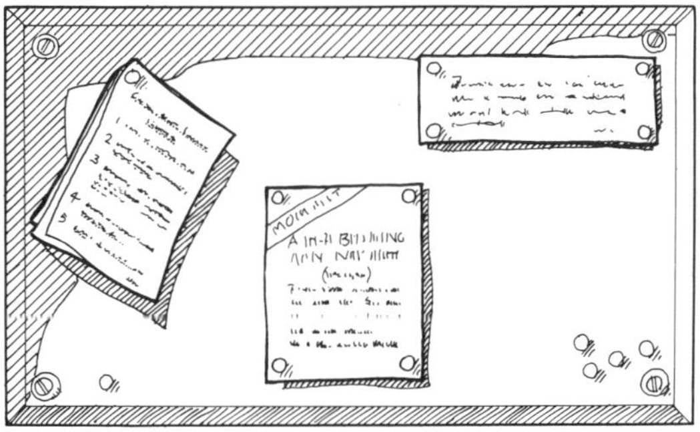

Three notices

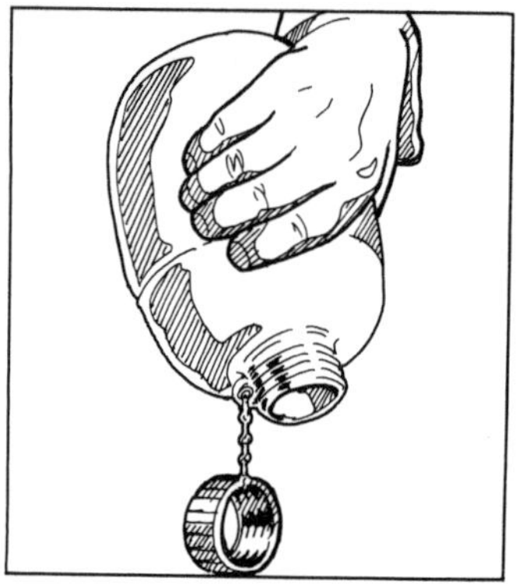

Exercise 1:4
Make negative sentences. For example:

There aren't any bottles.
There isn't any information.

Use these words:

jackets	water
clothing	rounds
equipment	items

Exercise 1:5
Ask questions about the countable and uncountable nouns. Notice for countable nouns we use 'How many . . . . .?' but for uncountable nouns we use 'How much . . . . .?'
For example:

How many bottles are there?
How much water is there?

Use these words:

rounds	notices	jackets
clothing	water	ammunition

D VOCABULARY

Reference List

ammunition (ammo)
bayonet
belt
boots
camouflage net
combat (jacket, trousers, kit, rations)
equipment
essential
face veil
fighting order
grenade (smoke, high explosive)
kit
machine gun
magazine
personal (weapon, kit)
pouches (front, rear)
rations
rifle
round (of ammunition)
section
sling
soldier
spare
steel helmet
uniform
water bottle
weapon

Exercise 1:6
Choose words from the Reference List which match the meanings below.

1. One piece of ammunition ....
2. Small bomb which you throw ....

3. Soldier's personal weapon ....
4. This is over the steel helmet ....
5. Food to eat when fighting ....
6. Very important – necessary ....
7. A small group of soldiers ....
8. A gun which can fire very quickly ....
9. Extra – not immediately needed ....
10. Containers for items of kit ....
11. Uniform for fighting in ....
12. Not a civilian ....

Exercise 1:7
Name these items of clothing, equipment and weapons.

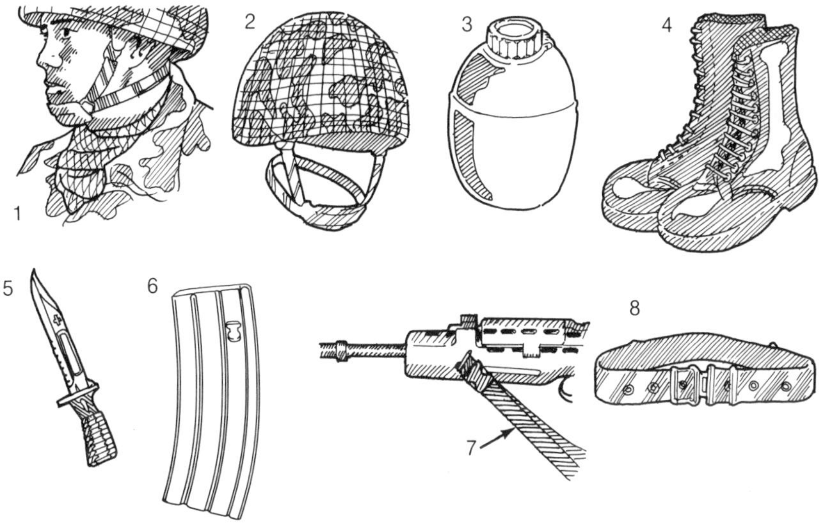

E DISCUSSION

Exercise 1:8
Protection from the weather is one good reason for wearing uniform. What other good reasons are there for wearing uniform?

What items of personal equipment are essential in fighting order?

UNIT 2

RECONNAISSANCE PATROL

A PRESENTATION

A reconnaissance (or recce) patrol must go to places where they can observe the enemy. Their task is to learn about the enemy's position, strength, activities, etc.

Lieutenant Edwards is in an observation post in a forward area close to the enemy. He is on a recce patrol with a corporal and two riflemen. Their task is to check a bridge across a river to see if it is safe for our tanks to cross. He is looking through binoculars.

B COMPREHENSION

Exercise 2:1

1. Where must the patrol go?
2. Why must they go there?
3. Is Lieutenant Edwards close to the enemy?
4. Who is he with?
5. What must he check?
6. Why must he check it?

Exercise 2:2
Read what Lieutenant Edwards is thinking and answer the questions.

'An enemy vehicle is approaching. It's a wheeled vehicle. It's stopping under those trees.'

1. What's happening?
2. What sort of vehicle is it?
3. Where's it stopping?

'Three men are getting out. One of them is an officer. A soldier is camouflaging the vehicle and the officer and the other soldier are moving towards the bridge.'

4. How many men are getting out?
5. Are they all officers?
6. What is one of the men doing?
7. Where are the other two men going?

'Now they are at the bridge. I think they are laying some explosive charges. I am continuing observation.'

8. Where are the enemy now?
9. What are they doing?
10. Is Lieutenant Edwards sure of this?
11. Has he stopped observing them?

C GRAMMAR FOCUS

What is the soldier doing?
He is camouflaging the vehicle. (or, *He's* camouflaging)
What are the men doing?
They are moving towards the bridge. (or, *They're* moving)

Exercise 2:3
Make a complete sentence to describe what is happening in each picture.

1

crawl across field

2

drive through water

3

lock papers in desk

4
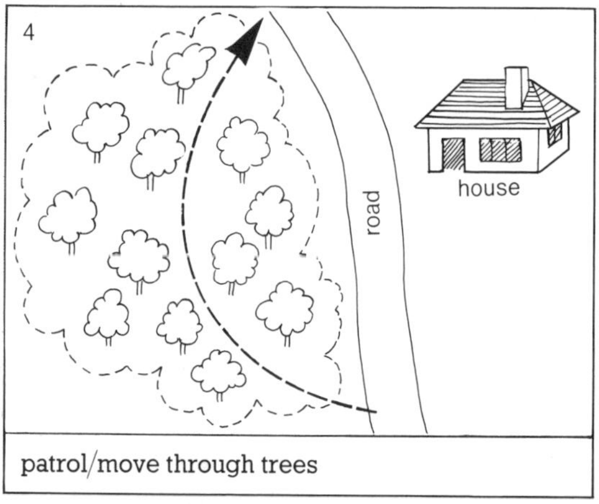

patrol/move through trees

5

run along road

6

eat their rations

Exercise 2:4
Look at the models:

Words:
They / check / bridge / task

They are checking the bridge. That is their task.

Words:
I / drive / vehicle / job

I am driving the vehicle. That is my job.

Now use these words:
They / check / bridge / task.

I / drive / vehicle / job.

You / check / ammunition / responsibility.

They / observe / enemy / task.

She / lock / papers / desk / responsibility.

He / camouflage / truck / task.

We / prepare / food / job.

D VOCABULARY

Reference List

activity (-ies)	forward area	reconnaissance
to approach	to lay (explosives)	responsibility
binoculars	lieutenant	rifleman
bridge	observation	river
to camouflage	observation post	safe
corporal	to observe	strength
to crawl	officer	tank
enemy	patrol	task
explosive charge	position	vehicle
field		

Exercise 2:5

Use words from the Reference List to complete the following sentences.

1. We are going to get information about the ________. (Not our friends.)
2. The commander wants to know their ________. (Number of men.)
3. The officer is in an ________ ________. (Place where he can see easily.)
4. The soldier is ________ his vehicle. (Making it hard to see.)
5. Sometimes, the best way to go across an open field is to ________. (Move face down on the ground.)
6. The enemy are in ________ under some trees. (Place.)
7. The officer can now report the ________ of the enemy. (Things they are doing.)
8. Lieutenant Edwards and his patrol are on ________. (Trying to get information about the enemy.)
9. The patrol's observation post is in a ________ ________. (Place close to the enemy.)
10. The enemy is ________ an explosive charge. (Putting it in position.)

Exercise 2:6
Use words from the Reference List to name the following.

1

2
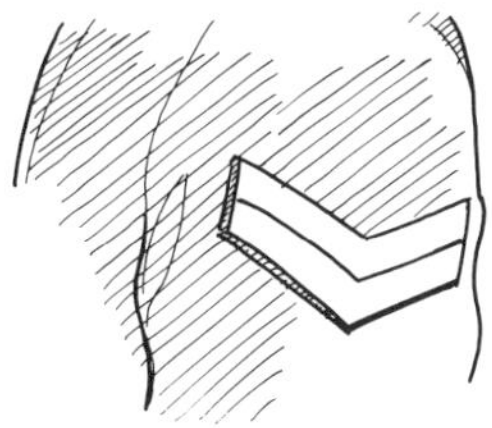

3

4

5
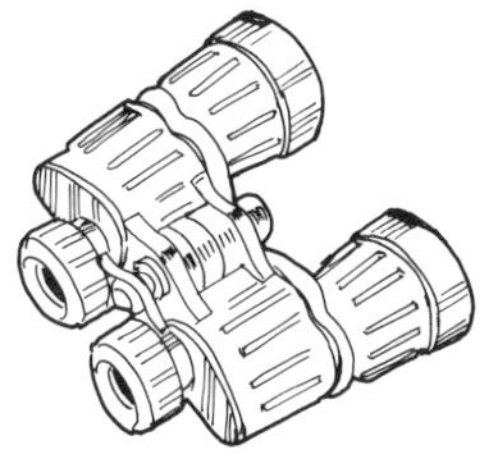

6

Exercise 2:7
Here are some military abbreviations that you will often see. Find the full words in the Reference List.

1. veh
2. str
3. OP
4. Lt
5. cam
6. recce
7. en
8. offr
9. rfn
10. br
11. posn
12. Cpl
13. ptl

E DISCUSSION

Exercise 2:8
Before you go on a recce patrol what information do you think you need? What equipment do you think you need?

UNIT 3

THE INFANTRY PLATOON

A PRESENTATION

An infantry platoon consists of about 30 men, with an officer in command. There is a platoon headquarters and there are three sections. Each section consists of about eight men, with a corporal in command.

Platoon headquarters
This is Lieutenant Edwards. He commands Number 3 Platoon. Six men work with him in the platoon headquarters.

Sergeant Wilson is the second-in-command. He helps Lt Edwards run the platoon.

Private Smith is the platoon's radio operator. He communicates with other platoons.

Sometimes Lt Edwards cannot use the radio. He has a runner, Private Carter, to take messages by hand.

These men operate the mortar. Private Brown carries the weapon. He is Number 1 on the mortar. Private White carries the mortar bombs. He is Number 2 on the mortar.

Finally, there is Private Jackson. He is a rifleman.

Everyone in the platoon headquarters carries a rifle as his personal weapon, except for Pte Smith and Pte White. Because they have heavy equipment to carry they each have a sub-machine gun as their personal weapon.

B COMPREHENSION

Exercise 3:1

1. How many men are there in a platoon?
2. How many men are there in a section?
3. What does Lt Edwards do?
4. How many men work with him in the platoon headquarters?
5. Who is the second-in-command?

6. What is Pte Smith's job?
7. Why does Lt Edwards need a runner?
8. What do Pte Brown and Pte White do?
9. Which man carries the mortar?
10. Which man carries the mortar bombs?
11. Which personal weapon does Pte Jackson carry?
12. Why do Pte Smith and Pte White have a sub-machine gun as their personal weapon?

C GRAMMAR FOCUS

What is his name? (or, *What's* his name?)
What does he do? He operates ......
Which personal weapon does he carry? He carries ......
Who commands the platoon? Lt Edwards does.
Does Lt Edwards command the platoon? Yes, he does.
Does Pte Jackson operate the radio? No, he doesn't.

Exercise 3:2
Look at the model:

Question 1: What is his name?
Answer 1: (His name is) Lt Edwards.
Question 2: What does he do?
Answer 2: He commands the platoon.
Question 3: Which personal weapon does he carry?
Answer 3: He carries a rifle.

Use these words to ask and answer questions.

1. Lt Edwards / commands the platoon / rifle.
2. Sgt Wilson / helps the platoon commander / rifle.
3. Pte Smith / operates the radio / sub-machine gun.
4. Pte Carter / takes messages by hand / rifle.
5. Pte Brown / { helps to operate the mortar
carries the mortar / } /rifle
6. Pte White / { helps to operate the mortar
carries the mortar bombs } /sub-machine gun
7. Pte Jackson / is a rifleman / rifle.

Exercise 3:3
Use the words in Exercise 3:2 to ask and answer 'Who?' questions. For example:

Question 1: Who commands the platoon?
Answer 1: Lt Edwards does.
Question 2: Who helps the platoon commander?
Answer 2: Sgt Wilson does.

Exercise 3:4

Notice: Lt Edwards commands the platoon.
Does Lt Edwards command the platoon?

Now ask and answer 'Yes/No' questions. For example:

Question 1: Does Lt Edwards command the platoon?
Answer 1: Yes, he does.
Question 2: Does Sgt Wilson operate the radio?
Answer 2: No, he doesn't.
Question 3: Do all the men carry a personal weapon?
Answer 3: Yes, they do.
Question 4: Do all the men carry a rifle?
Answer 4: No, they don't.

Words:

Lt Edwards / platoon.
Sgt Wilson / radio.
Pte Carter / messages by hand.
Pte Smith / mortar.
all the men / personal weapons.
all the men / rifle.
Pte Smith and Pte White / sub-machine gun.
Lt Edwards and Sgt Wilson / mortar.

D VOCABULARY

Reference List

battalion	to consist of	operator
bomb	headquarters	platoon
by hand	infantry	private
to command	message	radio
in command	mortar	runner
commander	Number 1, 2, etc. (on a weapon)	second-in-command
to communicate		sergeant
company	to operate	sub-machine gun

Exercise 3:5

Choose words from the Reference List which match the meanings below.

1. A unit which has three sections. ....
2. Soldiers who fight on foot. ....
3. The group which commands the unit. ....
4. A soldier who takes messages by hand. ....
5. A unit which has three platoons. ....

Exercise 3:6
Use words from the Reference List to complete the following sentences.

1. When the platoon commander is away his ________ ________ ________ is in charge.
2. The radio ________ is sending a message.
3. The section commanders must report to the lieutenant at platoon ________.
4. The platoon commander has a radio to ________ with other platoons.
5. A battalion usually ________ ________ five companies.
6. Two privates ________ the mortar.

Exercise 3:7
Use words from the Reference List to name the following:

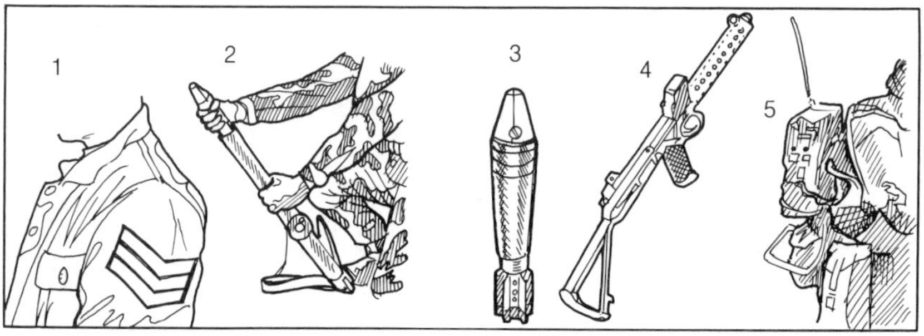

Exercise 3:8
Below are some military abbreviations that you will often see. Find the full words in the Reference List.

1. pl 2. bn 3. coy 4. Sgt 5. Pte 6. SMG 7. HQ
8. inf 9. msg 10. 2IC 11. comd 12. rad op 13. mor

E DISCUSSION

Exercise 3:9

This chart shows the organisation of an infantry battalion. You can see how the platoon fits in. How does this compare with the army in your country?

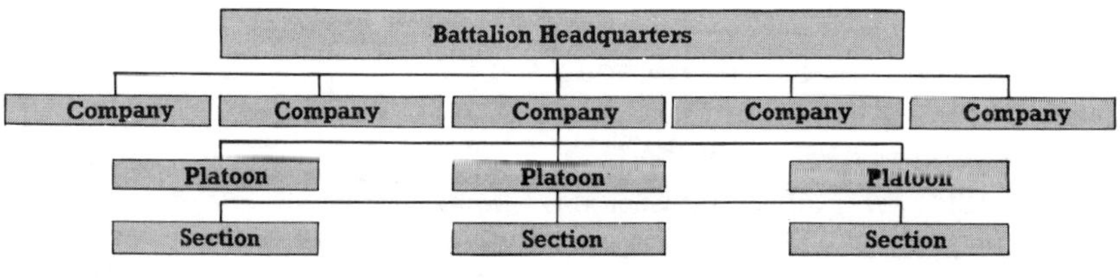

UNIT 4

RETURN TO HEADQUARTERS

A | PRESENTATION

The reconnaissance patrol is returning to Platoon Headquarters. Pte Jackson is in front. He is not far from the sentry who is in the foreground on the right. The other men are behind him. All of the men are on this side of the river. Lt Edwards is in the distance, between the bridge and the building. He is at the rear. The other two men are riflemen. There is a small tree to the left of one of them.

The sentry is challenging Pte Jackson:

'Halt! Who goes there?'

B | COMPREHENSION

Exercise 4:1

1. Where is the reconnaissance patrol returning to?
2. Who is in front?
3. Where is the sentry?
4. How many men are behind Pte Jackson?
5. Are the men on the far side of the river?
6. Where is Lt Edwards?
7. Where are the two riflemen?
8. What is there to the left of one of them?

Exercise 4:2
Read what the sentry does and answer the questions.

The sentry must know how to raise the alarm if he sees enemy troops. He challenges anyone who approaches his post. When there is a party of soldiers, the first one gives the password quietly in reply. He then stays with the sentry and identifies the other men as they approach one at a time.

1. What must the sentry know?
2. If anyone approaches his post what does he do?
3. What does the first man in the party do?
4. Does he stay with the sentry?
5. Do the other men in the party approach the sentry all together?

C GRAMMAR FOCUS

It's in front of / next to / behind (etc.) the building.

Exercise 4:3
Look at the picture and choose the correct words or phrases. For example:
Question 1: Which vehicle is shown in the picture?
Answer 1: It's an armoured personnel carrier.
Question 2: Where is it?
Answer 2: It's in front of the trees.

1. Which vehicle?

   truck?
   armoured personnel carrier?
   tank?

   in front of?
   behind?
   in the middle of?

2. Which weapon?

   mortar?
   sub-machine gun?
   rifle?

   behind?
   beside?
   far away from?

3. Which officer?

major?
captain?
lieutenant?

behind?
in front of?
to the left of?

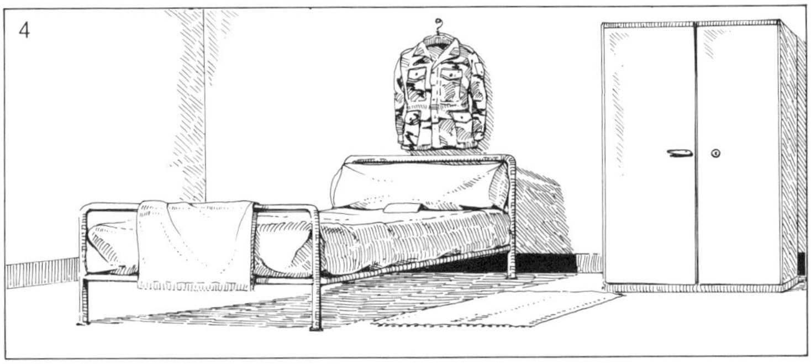

4. Which item of clothing?

combat jacket?
combat trousers?
face veil?

above?
beside?
below?

5. Which item of equipment?

binoculars?
radio?
water bottle?

on top of?
to the left of?
to the right of?

6. Which sub-unit?

section?
platoon?
company?

on this side?
on the far side?
half-way across?

D VOCABULARY

Reference List

to approach	to halt	post
armoured personnel carrier	major	to raise the alarm
captain	non-commissioned officer	rank
to challenge	officer	sentry
distance	party	troops
foreground	password	warrant officer

Exercise 4:4
Use words from the Reference List to complete the following sentences.

1. In front of the platoon headquarters was a ________. (Soldier watching for the enemy.)
2. He saw a ________ (Group.) of soldiers returning from patrol.
3. The patrol ________ (Came towards.) the sentry's ________. (Place of duty.)
4. His job was to ________ them. (See if they were friends or enemy.)
5. He ordered them to ________. (Stop.)
6. The first man had to give the ________. (Secret word.)
7. The patrol was friendly so the sentry did not need to ________ ________ ________. (Warn the rest of the headquarters.)
8. The next morning No. 2 Section moved forward in an ________ ________ ________. (Vehicle for carrying infantry.)
9. The Section Commander saw some enemy ________ (Soldiers.) in the ________. (A long way off.)
10. In the ________ (Close to) he saw a good position for the machine gun.

Exercise 4:5
Look at the picture.

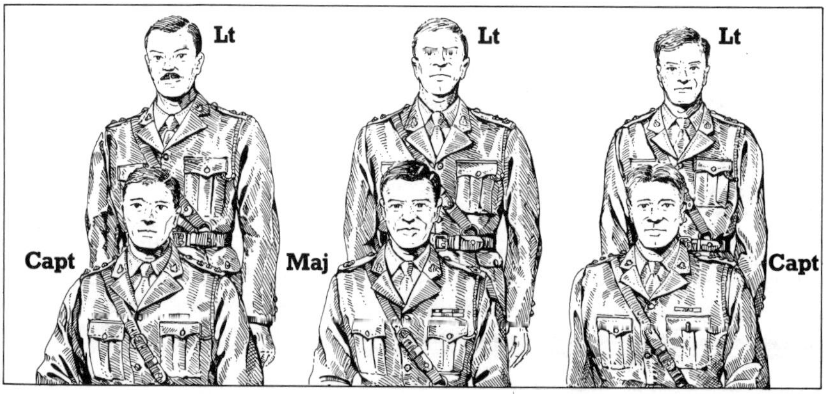

Use words from the Reference List to complete the following sentences.

1. All these men are ________.
2. There is one ________ in the picture.
3. There are two ________.
4. In the back row there are three lieutenants.
5. The man in the middle of the front row has the highest ________.

Exercise 4:6

Below are some military abbreviations that you will often see. Find the full words in the Reference List.

1. NCO
2. rk
3. APC
4. capt
5. maj
6. tps
7. WO

E DISCUSSION

Exercise 4:7

The British Army is divided into commissioned ranks and other ranks. The commissioned ranks are officers – such as lieutenants, captains, majors, etc. The other ranks are warrant officers (sergeant majors), non-commissioned officers (corporals, sergeants, etc.) and private soldiers (riflemen, privates). What is the rank structure of your army? How does it compare with the British Army?

How long do you think a sentry should stay on duty?
Why is it best to say the password quietly?
Can you think of some ways of raising the alarm if the enemy approaches your headquarters at night?

UNIT 5

AT THE INFORMATION POST

A PRESENTATION

The Brigade Headquarters is on exercise and is in a camouflaged position in a wood. Major Robinson is at the information post. This is at the entrance to the headquarters. He needs to know where the operations tent is. A corporal will give him this information.

First he speaks to the sentry.

Sentry: 'Good morning, sir. Identity, please.'
Major Robinson: 'Good morning. I'm Major Robinson. Here's my ID card. I have to report to the operations officer at 1000 hours.'
Sentry: 'Right, sir. Go into the information post and the corporal will show you where the operations tent is.'
Major Robinson: 'Good morning, corporal.'
Corporal: 'Good morning, sir. Can I help you?'

Major Robinson: 'How can I find the operations officer?'

Corporal: 'I'll just uncover the map for you, sir . . . . . . You are here. Go along this track to your left for about 100 metres. You'll see a footbridge over a stream to your right. Cross the footbridge and take the track to your right. After about 10 metres, you'll reach the operations tent. It's on your left-hand side hidden under the trees.'

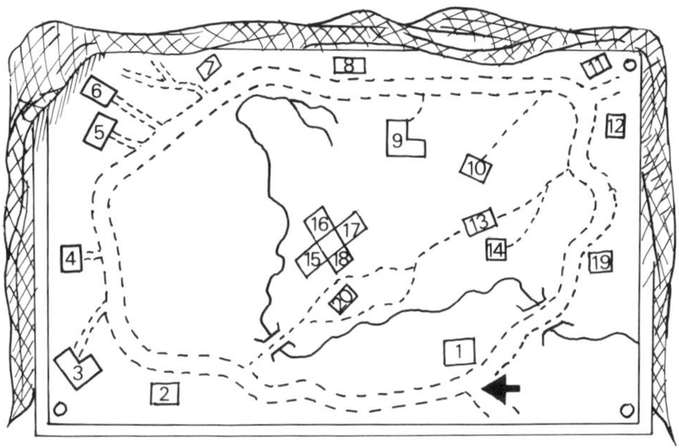

Major Robinson: 'Thanks, corporal. I'll be about an hour.'

Corporal: 'Very good, sir. Please report here again before you leave the headquarters.'

Major Robinson: 'O.K.'

B COMPREHENSION

Exercise 5:1

1. Is the Brigade Headquarters out in open ground?
2. What is at the entrance to the headquarters?
3. What does Major Robinson need to know?
4. Who does he speak to first, and what does he show him?
5. Which officer does he have to report to at 1000 hours?
6. What do the major and the corporal both look at?
7. How will Major Robinson cross the stream?
8. Which way will he turn after he has crossed the stream?
9. What does Major Robinson have to do before he leaves the headquarters?

C GRAMMAR FOCUS

Move along the hedge.
You will come to a barn.

Exercise 5:2
Make sentences from the tables for each of the pictures:

	along	the hedge.
	past	the barn.
Move	over	the footbridge.
Go	across	the road.
Keep	round	the village.
	through	the water.
	away from	the open ground.
	into	the forest.

		the barn.
	come to	the footbridge.
You will	see	the road.
(You'll)	reach	the village.
		the water.
		the open ground.
		the forest.

1

2

3

4

5

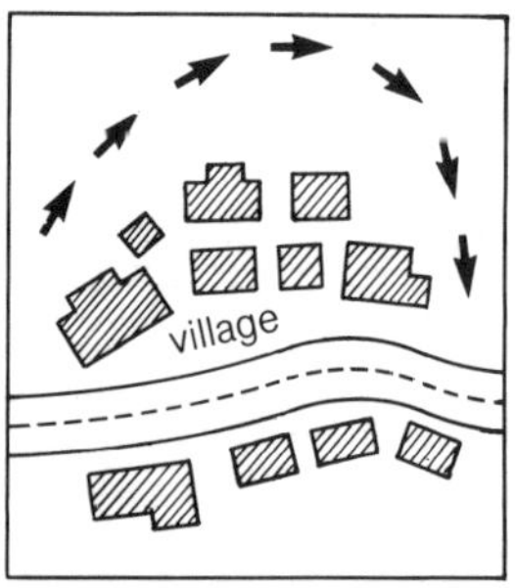

6

7

8

Exercise 5:3
Cover the sentences in Exercise 5:2. Look at the pictures and practise giving directions. Here are some useful words and phrases:
Soon
After a while
After 100 metres
as quickly as possible
without being seen

Here are some sentences to help you:
Move along the hedge.
Soon you will come to a barn.
Go past the barn.
After 100 metres you will see a footbridge.
Now continue . . .

D VOCABULARY

Reference List

barn	hedge	operations
brigade	identity card	to report (to a person or place)
exercise	information post	stream
footbridge	map	track
forest	open ground	village

Exercise 5:4
Use words from the Reference List to complete the following sentences.

1. The sentry checked the major's ________ ________.
2. The corporal showed the major the position of the operations tent on the ________.
3. A ________ is a large group of soldiers which consists of more than three battalions.
4. You can get answers to questions about the headquarters at the ________ ________.
5. The brigade commander has an ________ officer to help him plan the fighting.
6. The brigade is not fighting a real battle. It is on ________ to practise its officers and soldiers.
7. 'The platoon commander wants to see you, Lance-corporal Evans. ________ to him at 1130 hours this morning,' said the sergeant.

Exercise 5:5
Look at the picture. It shows the ground which is in front of No 2 Section. The Section Commander has done a recce of the ground. He is briefing his section. Complete his description of the ground by using words from the Reference List.

Section commander's briefing
'Across our front is a road. The nearest ________ is 2 miles to our left. Over the road and also across our front is a ________. This is crossed by a ________. A ________ goes from the road and leads to a ________. On the left-hand side of this is a long low ________. In the distance is a ________ which will give good cover. Between this and the road there is no cover. We will be in ________ ________.'

Exercise 5:6
Here are some military abbreviations that you will often see. Find the full words in the Reference List.

1. ID	3. ex	5. bde
2. rep	4. ops	6. info

E DISCUSSION

Exercise 5:7
Why are information posts necessary? What do you think the sentry's duties are? What equipment would you need in an information post as well as a map?

BATTLE CAMP

A PRESENTATION

Once a year each platoon must attend training at Deacon Bridge Battle Camp. The platoon stays there for six days. This is their programme:

Monday
The men arrive at Deacon Bridge Battle Camp. They draw stores and equipment. Then they receive training in fighting in built-up areas.

Tuesday
They march to the battle simulation area. The section commanders take their sections over the battle simulation assault course.

Wednesday
This is the range day. The men march to the live-firing range and carry out live-firing of all platoon weapons.

Thursday
On Thursday they receive instruction in survival skills. Then they practise what they have learnt. For example, they build shelters and find food and water. They move around without being seen.

Friday
On Friday there is an exercise in which camp staff instructors act as the enemy. In the evening there is a demonstration of night patrolling skills and a practical exercise.

Saturday
On Saturday the men are free in the morning to rest and clean up the camp. In the afternoon there is an inter-section battle skills competition.

B COMPREHENSION

Exercise 6:1

1. How often must each platoon attend training at the Battle Camp?
2. How long do they stay there?
3. What is the first thing they do after they arrive?
4. What sort of training do they receive on Monday?
5. On Tuesday, how do they travel to the battle simulation area?
6. What do they practise on Wednesday?
7. What training will help them in the cold, the wind and the rain?
8. Who plays the part of the enemy on Friday?
9. Are they free on Friday evening?
10. What is there on Saturday afternoon?

C GRAMMAR FOCUS

The exercise starts at 0900 hours.
It lasts for six hours.
It finishes at 1500 hours.

Exercise 6:2
Look at the extract from the Battle Camp Programme.

Look at the model:
Question 1: When does the inspection start?
Answer 1: It starts at 0745 hours.
Question 2: How long does it last?
Answer 2: It lasts for fifteen minutes.
Question 3: When does it finish (end)?
Answer 3: It ends at 0800 hours.

Use these words:
inspection
briefing
demonstration
the first exercise
the second exercise
competition

FRIDAY

0745-0800	INSPECTION BY SECTION COMMANDERS AND PLATOON COMMANDER
0800-0830	BRIEFING FOR EXERCISE
0900-1500	EXERCISE WITH CAMP STAFF INSTRUCTORS AS ENEMY
1800-1900	DEMONSTRATION OF NIGHT PATROLLING SKILLS
1900-2230	PRACTICAL EXERCISE

SATURDAY

MORNING	FREE FOR REST AND CLEAN UP
1330-1730	INTER-SECTION BATTLE SKILLS COMPETITION

Exercise 6:3
Complete these sentences using the following words:

at on from until for

1. The Battle Camp training lasts ________ six days.
2. The men arrive at Deacon Bridge Battle Camp ________ Monday.
3. The demonstration starts ________ 1800 hours.
4. It lasts ________ 1800 hours ________ 1900 hours.
5. The men have a competition ________ the last day.
6. It lasts ________ four hours.
7. Soldiers work very hard ________ the start ________ the end of their training.
8. They usually leave the camp ________ about 1900 hours ________ Saturday.

D VOCABULARY

Reference List

assault course	to draw stores	shelter
battle	inspection	simulation
briefing	instruction	skills
built-up area	instructor	staff
camp	live-firing	stores
competition	to march	survival
demonstration	range	training

Exercise 6:4
Choose words from the Reference List which match the meanings below.

1. To go on foot ....
2. Shooting real ammunition ....
3. A teacher in the army ....
4. Staying alive in a dangerous situation ....
5. To collect kit and sign for it ....
6. Giving information about a task ....
7. Just like the real thing ....
8. It shows you how to do something ....
9. A test to see who is best ....
10. Teaching in the army ....
11. A large-scale fight ....
12. Things like rations, ammunition, tents, etc. ....
13. The people who run the camp ....
14. Checking of soldiers' kit, etc. ....
15. Things that a soldier must know and do very well ....
16. Learning and practising how to be a soldier ....

Exercise 6:5
Name the following places from the Reference List.

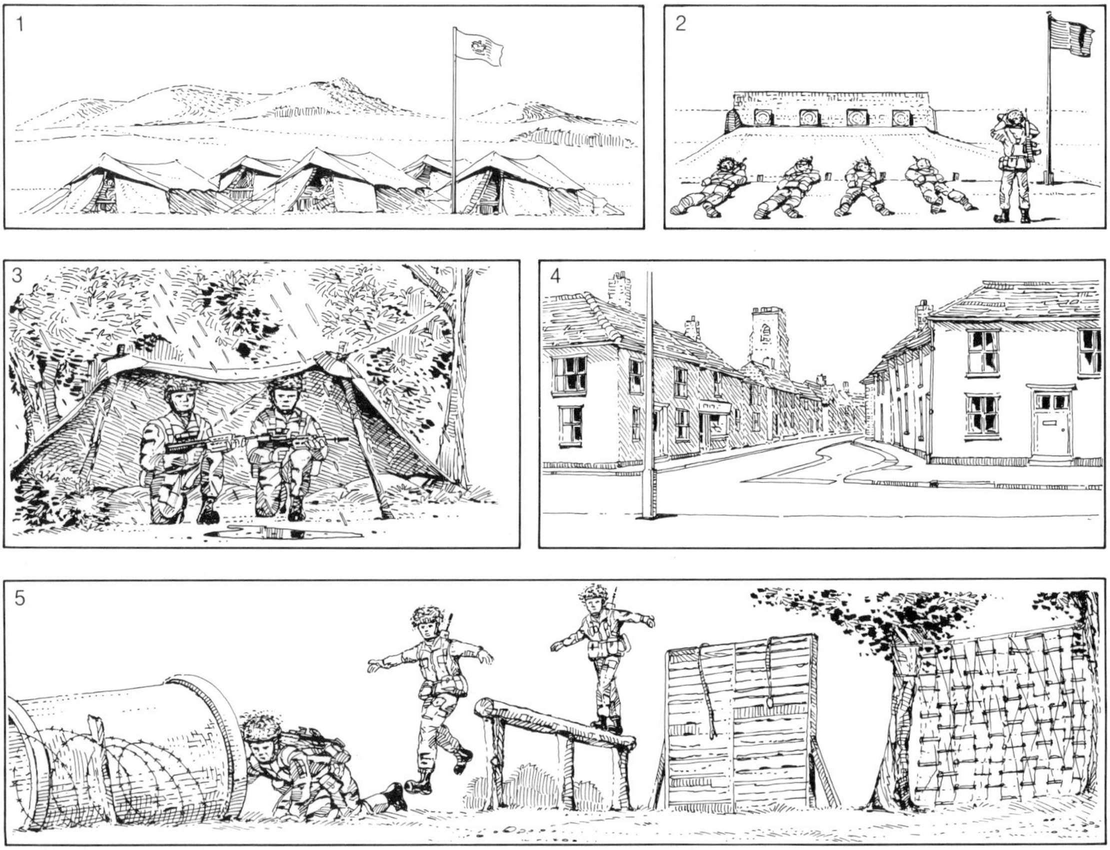

Exercise 6:6
Below are some military abbreviations that you will often see. Find the full words in the Reference List.

1. demo
2. instr
3. trg
4. asslt

E DISCUSSION

Exercise 6:7
What other kinds of training can you think of that would be useful at a Battle Camp? Do you think one week's training a year in battle skills is enough?

WEAPON HANDLING

A	PRESENTATION

Sgt Ford is giving a lesson on weapon handling.
'All weapons are lethal. That means they can kill you. One of the most important things in weapon training is knowing the rules of safety. We call these "normal safety precautions". Soldiers who don't follow these rules are very dangerous. They can wound or accidentally kill their friends.
Here are the main rules. Listen carefully.

- Always point your rifle in a safe direction. Don't point it at another person unless you intend to kill him. It makes no difference if the rifle is loaded or not.
- Don't load your rifle unless you have to.
- Don't play with the trigger. Keep your finger off the trigger if it doesn't have to be there.
- Keep the safety catch applied. Don't release it unless you're going to fire the rifle.
- Assume that a weapon is loaded until you have cleared it. Always unload it and clear it as soon as possible. Make sure that it is clear if you hand it to anyone.
- Keep close to your rifle. Don't leave it unattended. Don't rest it against walls, for example, or the sides of vehicles.

These are the main points I want to make about normal safety precautions. Are there any questions?'

B COMPREHENSION

Exercise 7:1

1. In weapon training, what are rules of safety called?
2. Why must soldiers follow these rules?
3. Which way should you point your rifle?
4. Does it make any difference if the rifle is unloaded?
5. What must you not do with the trigger?
6. When may you release the safety catch?
7. Is it all right to assume that a weapon is unloaded?
8. What must you do before you hand a weapon to someone?
9. Where must you not rest your rifle?

C GRAMMAR FOCUS

Listen carefully.
Don't (Do not) point your rifle at your friend.
Show the rifle to the sergeant.
Show the sergeant the rifle.

Exercise 7:2
Look at the models:

L listen carefully.
Don't point the rifle at your friend.

Now complete these sentences by using a capital letter or 'Don't' as appropriate:

1. ...... listen carefully.
2. ...... point the rifle at your friend.
3. ...... play with the trigger.
4. ...... keep the safety catch applied unless you are going to fire.
5. ...... unload the rifle as soon as possible.
6. ...... show that the rifle is empty when handing it to someone else.
7. ...... rest it against vehicles.
8. ...... keep close to your rifle.
9. ...... load your rifle unless you have to.
10. ...... forget to follow normal safety precautions.

Exercise 7:3
Choose the rule for each of these five pictures.

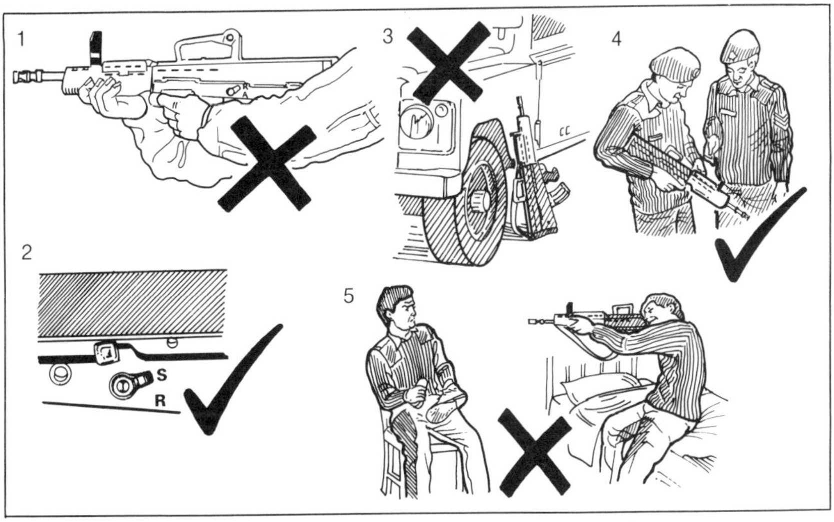

Exercise 7:4
Look at the model:
Show the rifle to the sergeant.
Show the sergeant the rifle.

Now use these words to make sentences:
show / rifle / sergeant.
give / password / sentry.
send / message / headquarters.
hand / binoculars / lieutenant.
send / information / instructors.
show / map / Major Robinson.
send / stores / Battle Camp.
give / papers / officer in charge.

D VOCABULARY

Reference List

to apply (safety catch)
to assume
to clear
clear
lethal
loaded/unloaded
precautions (safety precautions)
to release (safety catch)
safety catch
trigger
weapon handling

Exercise 7:5
Use words from the Reference List to complete the following sentences.

1. The sergeant ________ the weapon. (Checked to make sure it was empty and safe.)
2. All weapons are ________. (Able to kill.)
3. ________ the safety catch until you wish to fire. (Make sure the safety catch is on.)
4. You cannot fire unless you ________ the safety catch. (Push it to the off position.)
5. Never ________ that a weapon is safe. (Believe without checking first.)
6. The instructor was teaching weapon ________. (How to use weapons correctly and safely.)
7. All soldiers must know the ________ ________________ for the rifle. (Rules of safety.)

Exercise 7:6
Below is a picture of a rifle. Names of some of its parts which are new to you have been put in. Try to name the other parts with words you should already know.

1. Rifle cannot fire when it is applied. ______________________
2. Knife attached to the muzzle. ______________________
3. This holds the ammunition. ______________________
4. When you pull this the rifle fires. ______________________
5. Used for carrying the rifle. ______________________

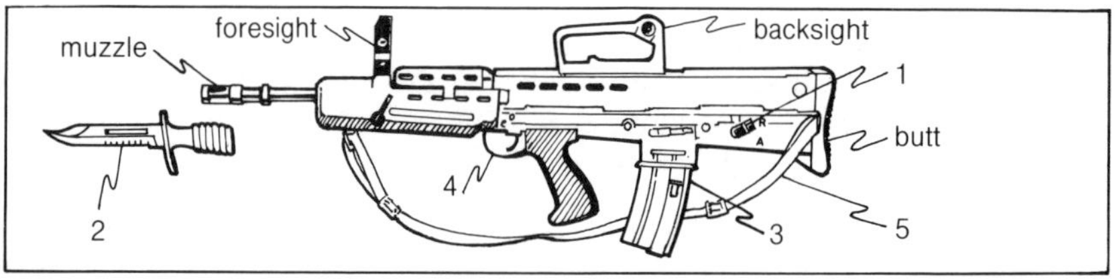

Question
In the picture above is the rifle loaded or unloaded? (Give a reason for your answer.)

E DISCUSSION

Exercise 7:7
What would you do in the following situations?

You are on an exercise and you find a rifle leaning against your vehicle.

Another soldier asks you to hold his rifle while he camouflages an APC.

UNIT 8

FIT TO FIGHT

A PRESENTATION

A soldier must be fit. If he is unfit, he can't do his job properly and he lets his comrades down. He may endanger their lives.

He must train every day to improve his fitness. He does exercises in the gym to develop his agility, strength and endurance.

He trains on the assault course. At first this is easy, but it gets more and more difficult.

Also he trains in simulated battle conditions. He carries his weapons and equipment and uses them in noisy conditions, under fire, and in bad weather.

The men of No 3 Platoon are having a competition. They are tested for fitness and also in military skills such as shooting, attack and ambush drills, and night patrolling. The most important test of their fitness is the ten-mile endurance march. They have to run and march ten miles in fighting order in their best time. There is a prize for the first one to finish.

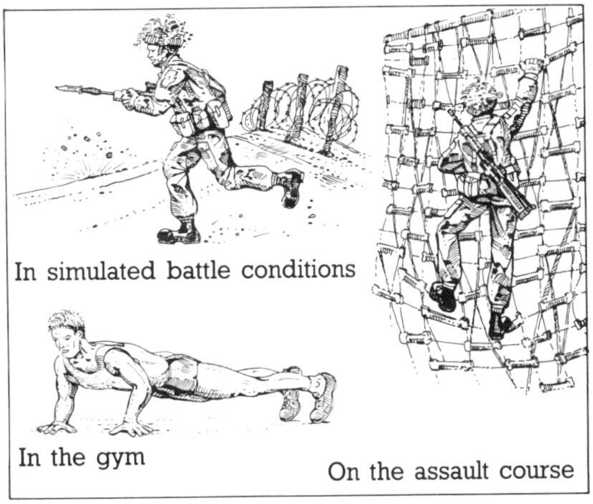

In simulated battle conditions

In the gym

On the assault course

Here are Pte Smith and Pte Jackson. They are finishing the march. They both want to be the first to return to the headquarters. Pte Smith is on the right. He is older than Pte Jackson and he is not quite so agile. Pte Jackson is a faster runner than Pte Smith is. However, Smith is bigger and stronger than Jackson is. He has greater powers of endurance.

Endurance march

Pte Smith is the first man to finish.

He is the fittest man in the platoon.

B COMPREHENSION

Exercise 8:1

1. Why must a soldier be fit?
2. Which three kinds of fitness must he develop?
3. Is the training on the assault course always the same?
4. In which ways are simulated battle conditions just like the real thing?
5. What sort of military skills are No 3 Platoon tested in?
6. What distance do the men cover on the march?
7. Which of the two privates is more agile than the other?
8. Which man is stronger?
9. Who is the fittest man in the platoon?

C GRAMMAR FOCUS

Pte Smith is older than Pte Jackson.
Pte Jackson is not as fit as Pte Smith.
Pte Smith is the fittest man in the platoon.

Exercise 8:2

Look at the model:

The river is deeper than the stream.
The stream is not as deep as the river.

Now look at the pictures and make similar sentences:

deep

low high

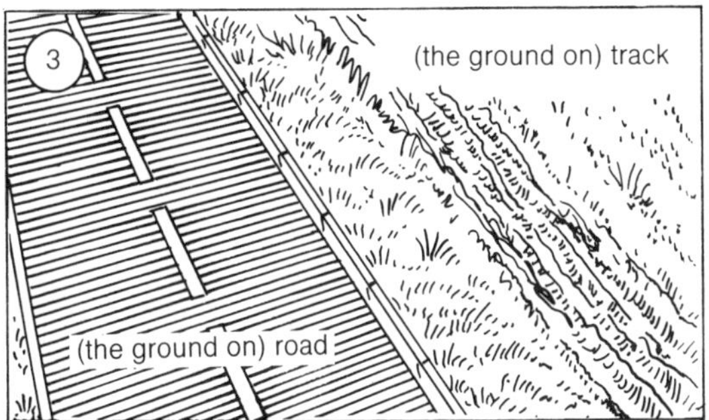

soft rough firm hard

big large small

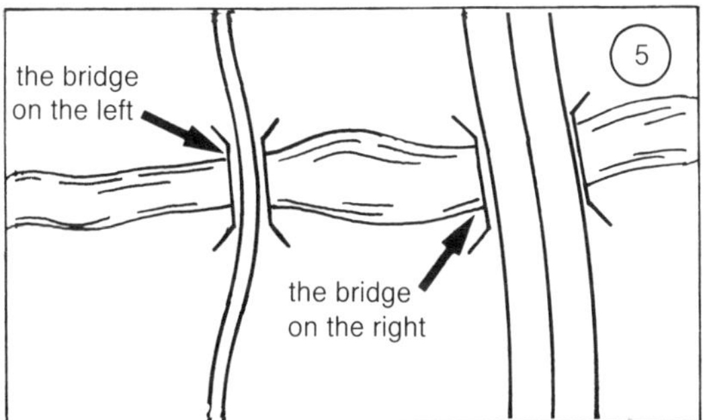

narrow wide

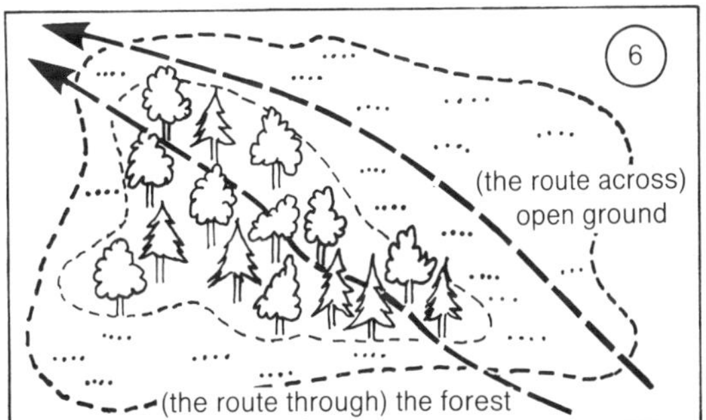

safe

Exercise 8:3

Rank	*Name*	*Age*	*Height*	*Weight*
Pte	Smith	21	5 ft 10 ins	12 st
Pte	Carter	20	5 ft 11 ins	12½ st
Pte	Brown	23	5 ft 9 ins	13 st
Pte	White	20	5 ft 6 ins	10½ st
Pte	Jackson	19	5 ft 8 ins	11 st

Look at the models:
Pte Jackson is younger than Pte Brown.
Pte Brown is taller than Pte White.
Pte Brown is the heaviest man in the group.
Now make similar sentences from the table.

How old is Pte Smith?
How heavy is Pte Brown?
How long is the trench?
What is the length of the trench?

Exercise 8:4
Look at the models:
Question 1: How old is Pte Smith?
Answer 1: He's 21 years old.
Question 2: How heavy is Pte Brown?
Answer 2: He's 13 stone. *or* He weighs 13 stone.

Now look at the table again and ask and answer questions about the soldiers.

Exercise 8:5
As part of the competition in military skills the men must dig a trench . . . . . .

Look at the model:
Question: How long is the trench? *or*
What is the length of the trench?
Answer: It's 6 feet long.
Now ask and answer questions about the trench and the nearby hedge.

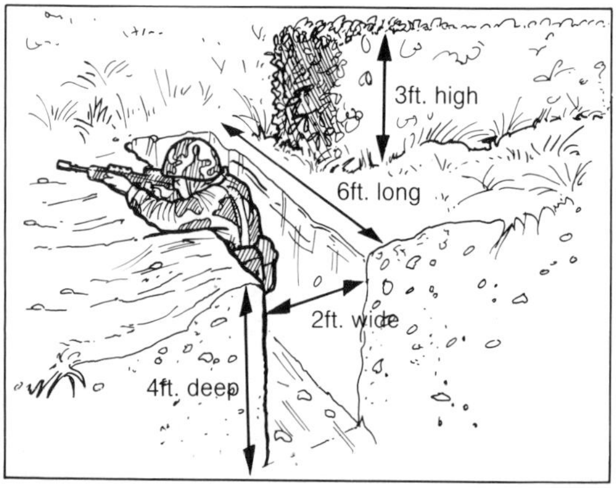

D VOCABULARY

Reference List	
agile/agility	fit/unfit
ambush/to ambush	fitness
comrade	gym (gymnasium)
to cover (ground)	stone (weight – 1 st. = about $6\frac{1}{2}$ kilos)
to endanger	trench
endurance	under fire (to be . . . to come . . . under fire)

Exercise 8:6

Choose words from the Reference List which match the meanings below.

1. To put someone in a situation where they could be killed ....
2. Place for practising physical exercises ....
3. A person you work with in the army ....
4. Ability to climb, jump, balance, etc. ....
5. Ability to do hard physical work for a long time ....

Exercise 8:7

Complete the following sentences using words from the Reference List.

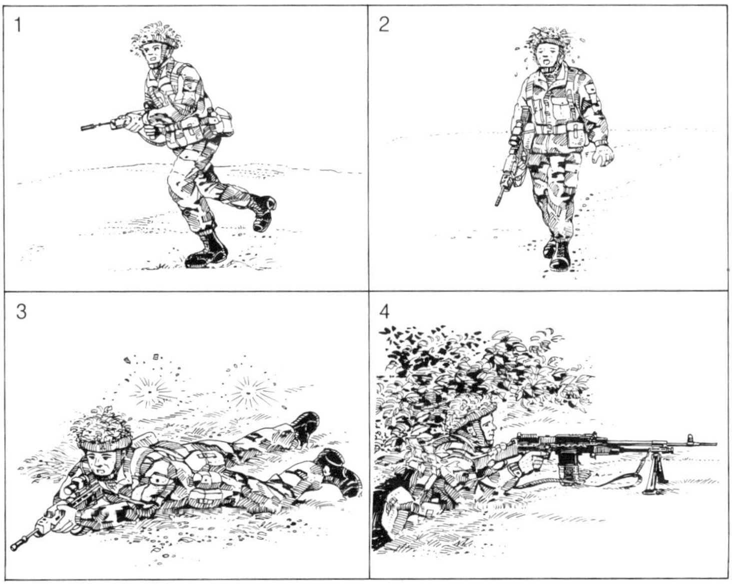

1. This soldier is ________. He can ________ the ground quickly.
2. This soldier weighs $17\frac{1}{2}$ ________. He is un________.
3. This soldier is ________ ________ from the enemy.
4. This soldier is in a ________. He is hiding and waiting to shoot the enemy when they come past his position. He is going to ________ them.

E DISCUSSION

Exercise 8:8
How much do you think fighting order weighs? (You may want to look at Unit 1 again.) What do you think would be a good time for a soldier to cover ten miles in fighting order? (Remember, he should be fit to fight at the end.)

UNIT 9

THE TANK

A PRESENTATION

The tank has certain characteristics which make it a good fighting machine.

It is armour-plated. This gives **protection** to the crew inside it.

It has a very large gun. This gives it **firepower**.

Although it is not very fast, it can travel across country. It does not have wheels; it has tracks. This gives it **mobility**.

The tank can be used in a number of different ways. It can fight on its own or in support of infantry, when moving or when standing still. It has **flexibility**.

The tank's weapons
The main armament on this tank is a gun. This has a calibre of 120 millimetres. It also has two machine guns. One of these is fixed beside the main armament. The other is at the top of the tank for use against enemy aircraft. On each side of the tank there are five smoke dischargers. These can throw smoke grenades to make a smoke screen so the tank can move without being seen.

Other details
The tank weighs 52 tonnes. Its top speed is only 30 miles per hour. The crew consists of the commander, the gunner, the driver and a fourth man who has two jobs. He loads the gun and operates the radio.

B COMPREHENSION

Exercise 9:1

1. What does the armour-plating on a tank give to the crew?
2. What gives the tank firepower?
3. Why is a tank able to travel across country?
4. Is there only one way in which a tank can be used?
5. What is the calibre of the main armament?
6. Which weapon can be used against enemy aircraft?
7. How many smoke dischargers are there on each side?
8. What can the smoke dischargers do?
9. How heavy is the tank?
10. What is its top speed?
11. How many men are there in the crew?

C GRAMMAR FOCUS

What has it got? ***or*** **What does it have?**
It has (got) a 120 millimetre gun.
What can it do?
It can travel across country.
A modern tank is more powerful than an older one.

Exercise 9:2
Make sentences from the tables.

1. *What sort of vehicle is it?*

It	is	a tank. a good fighting machine. very heavy. not very fast.

2. *What has the tank got?*

It	has (got)	a 120 millimetre gun. two machine guns. five smoke dischargers on each side.

3. *What can the tank do?*

It	can	travel fight support move fire	across country. on its own. the infantry. under cover of a smokescreen. when moving or standing still.

Exercise 9:3
An old tank and a modern tank.

Look at the models:
It costs a lot of money to produce a modern tank. (**expensive**)
A modern tank is more expensive than an old one.
A modern tank has a big engine. (**powerful**)
A modern tank is more powerful than an old one.

Words – The tanks:
1. It costs a lot of money to produce a modern tank. (**expensive**)
2. A modern tank has a big engine. (**powerful**)
3. It can travel across ground which an old one could not cover. (**mobile**)
4. There are fewer problems with a modern tank. (**reliable**)
5. The crew in an old tank could be hit more easily. (**vulnerable**)

Words – The main armament:

6. In an old tank, the gun went up and down with the vehicle. A modern tank has a gun which stays on the target. (**stable**)
7. The new gun usually hits the target. (**accurate**)
8. The new gun is much bigger. (**powerful**)

D VOCABULARY

Reference List			
accurate	cupola	modern	smoke screen
aircraft	firepower	protection	stable
armament	flexibility	reliable	support
armour	hull	smoke discharger	tank
armour-plated	machine	smoke grenade	tracks
calibre	mobility		vulnerable
characteristics			

Exercise 9:4

Choose words from the Reference List which match the meanings below.

1. A gun's size measured in millimetres ....
2. Thick metal protection ....
3. New, up-to-date ....
4. An engine or a vehicle ....
5. An aeroplane, helicopter, etc. ....
6. Nearly always hits the target ....
7. Easy to defeat ....
8. Will not break down easily ....
9. Help, assistance ....
10. Thing for throwing smoke grenades ....
11. What a smoke grenade can make ....
12. Firm, not moving about ....

Exercise 9:5

Choose words from the Reference List to complete the table. (If necessary read the Presentation text again.)

	Descriptions	*Characteristics*
1.	The tank has very good cross-country capability because of its tracks.	mobility
2.	The tank has a very large gun.	
3.	The tank is armour-plated.	
4.	The tank can be used in many different ways.	

Exercise 9:6
Below is a picture of a tank. After you have read the sentences, fill in the boxes.

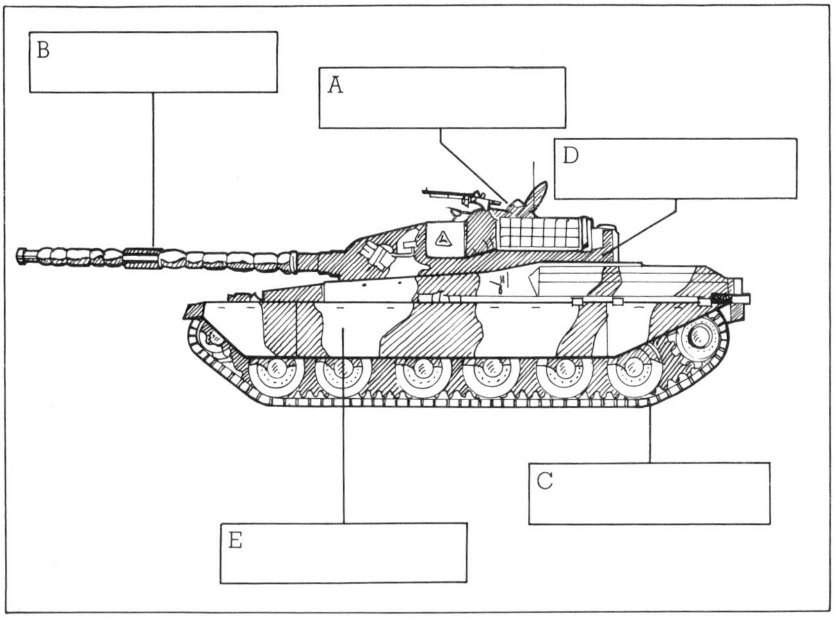

1. Find the **main armament**.
2. Find the **tracks**.
3. The main body of the tank is called the **hull**.
4. The part which has the main armament in it is called the **turret**.
5. On the top of the turret is the place for the commander. This is called the **cupola**.

Exercise 9:7
Here are some military abbreviations that you will often see. Find the full words in the Reference List.

1. tk	3. cal	5. smk
2. sp	4. ac	6. mob

E DISCUSSION

Exercise 9:8
How many different kinds of weapon can you think of which can be used to defeat a tank?

Can you think of any disadvantages that a tank has? (Here are some clues which might help you – *fuel – weight – air attack – cost – thick forest, mountains – crew.*)

UNIT 10

SURVIVAL IN THE FIELD

A PRESENTATION

A soldier must be able to look after himself properly. If he is wet, cold, tired and hungry, he cannot fight as well as a soldier who is dry, warm, rested and well-fed. Each individual soldier must learn the simple skills that help him to survive in the field.

Pte Allen is using his poncho to make a shelter. This will protect him from the weather and let him rest when he can.

1

Here he is eating his rations. He eats his food hot when he can. Sometimes he cannot light a fire because smoke and the smell of cooking might give his position away to the enemy.

2

Because he is thirsty he is going to take some water from a stream. Before he drinks it he will use a sterilising kit to ensure that it is clean. If he drinks dirty water he might become very ill.

3

He cut his hand on some barbed wire. Now he is covering the injury with a clean dressing.

4

Pte Allen wants to make sure that the enemy cannot see his position. He is using a net and some branches from the trees to camouflage his shelter.

5

He does not want the enemy to hear him so he makes as little noise as possible. A soldier in the field tries to move quietly and carefully at all times.

B COMPREHENSION

Exercise 10:1

1. Why is Pte Allen using his poncho to make a shelter?
2. Why is it sometimes dangerous to light a fire?
3. How will he make sure the stream water is clean?
4. What might happen if he drinks dirty water?
5. How did he cut his hand?
6. What is he putting on the injury?
7. Why is he camouflaging his shelter?
8. How is he doing this?
9. What must a soldier in the field try to do?
10. Why does a soldier learn these simple skills?

C GRAMMAR FOCUS

He is using his poncho to make a shelter.
He is covering the injury with a dressing.
Move quietly! You're not moving quietly enough.

Exercise 10:2
Look at the model:
He is using his poncho to make a shelter.
He is making a shelter with his poncho.
Now look at the pictures and make similar sentences.

1

make

2

clean

3

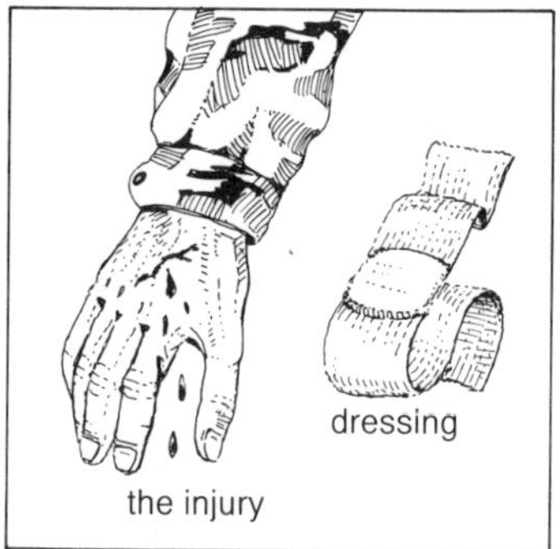

cover

4

camouflage

5

dig

6

hide

7

observe

8

cut

Exercise 10:3

Look at the model:

Move quietly! You're not moving quietly enough.

Now read the commands below and make similar sentences.

1. Move quietly!
2. Tie it securely!
3. Speak clearly!
4. Measure it accurately!
5. Sterilise it thoroughly!
6. Drive slowly!
7. Work quickly!
8. Check them carefully!

D VOCABULARY

Reference List

barbed wire	in the field	shovel
to dig	machete	to sterilise/sterilising kit
dressing	to measure	to survive/survival
injury	poncho	to tie

Exercise 10:4

Choose words from the Reference List which match the meanings below.

1. To find the size of something ....
2. To make a hole in the ground ....
3. To make very clean ....
4. To fasten together with rope or string ....
5. To stay alive in a dangerous situation ....
6. A broken leg, for example ....
7. Opposite of 'in barracks' ....
8. Equipment used to clean dirty water ....

Exercise 10:5
Use words from the Reference List to name the following.

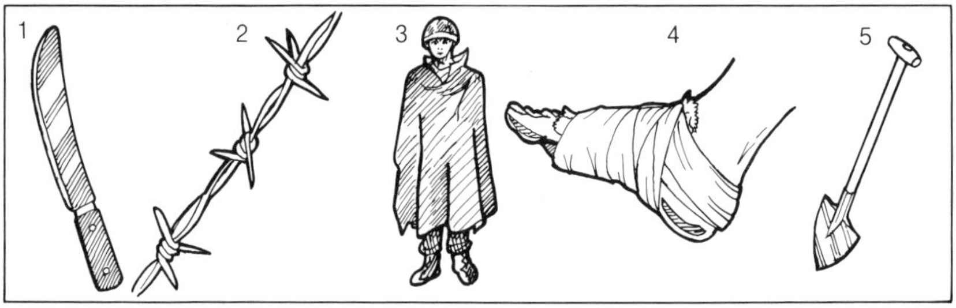

E DISCUSSION

Exercise 10:6
What other skills can you think of that would help a soldier to survive in the field? Which of these skills do you think are the most important?

PROGRESS TEST 1 (Units 1–5)

Read the following sentences and choose the best answer.

1. A platoon consists of ________
   a) a coy. b) three sects. c) about ten men.
2. Lt Smith is a pl comd and ________ Jones is his 2IC.
   a) Capt b) Sgt c) Cpl
3. Lt Smith is looking at the enemy from an ________
   a) OP. b) ops tent. c) info post.
4. He is on a recce patrol. His task is to ________ a) lay explosive charges. b) communicate with the en. c) see where the en are.
5. Some soldiers are far away ________
   a) beside him. b) in the distance. c) in the foreground.
6. He is looking at them ________ binoculars.
   a) in b) through c) in front of
7. If they are ________ I must raise the alarm.
   a) our soldiers b) some of our men c) en tps
8. I must know who you are: show me your ________
   a) maps. b) ID card. c) personal eqpt.
9. The soldiers are in fighting order. They are wearing ________ round their necks
   a) face veils b) belts c) slings
10. One of the men is carrying the ________ for the machine gun.
    a) bayonet b) grenades c) spare rounds
11. No 1 and No 2 on the mortar are carrying the ________ as their personal wpn.
    a) rifle b) mortar c) SMG
12. How much ammo ________
    a) there is? b) is there? c) are there?
13. The ________ which the men are in is a truck.
    a) APC b) vehicle c) tank
14. You must keep down. ________ across the field!
    a) Walk b) Run c) Crawl
15. Walk ________ the water.
    a) through b) along c) under

PROGRESS TEST 2 (Units 6–10)

Read the following sentences and choose the best answer.

1. On a range day the men ________
   a) carry out live firing. b) march to the battle simulation area. c) act as the enemy.
2. The men have a practical exercise in night patrolling skills ________ these have been demonstrated.
   a) before b) after c) until
3. Don't load your rifle ________ you have to.
   a) because b) if c) unless
4. Keep close to your rifle: don't ________
   a) keep the safety catch applied. b) leave it unattended. c) assume it is loaded.
5. The soldier uses ________ to carry the rifle.
   a) the sling b) the barrel c) the muzzle
6. The trench is ________
   a) six feet. b) six feet long. c) six feet length.
7. Soldiers are tested in ________ such as shooting, attack and ambush drills.
   a) battle conditions b) night patrolling c) military skills
8. The tank is armour-plated. This gives it ________
   a) mobility. b) protection. c) firepower.
9. A tank can use its ________ to move without being seen.
   a) main armament b) tracks c) smoke dischargers
10. A modern tank is ________ an old one.
    a) more powerful than b) not as powerful as c) less powerful than
11. The gun usually hits the target: it is ________
    a) powerful. b) flexible. c) accurate.
12. The smell of cooking ________ give away his position.
    a) must b) might c) will not
13. He is using ________ to cut the branch.
    a) barbed wire b) a machete c) a shovel
14. Because of his poncho he will not get ________
    a) tired. b) hungry. c) wet.
15. Sterilise it ________
    a) accurately. b) thoroughly. c) securely.

UNIT 11

ROOM INSPECTIONS

A PRESENTATION

Last night Pte Thomas prepared his room for inspection.

Here are some of the things he had to do.

He swept the floor, shook out the mat and emptied the waste bin. He cleaned the wash area and laid out his toiletry items carefully. He made the bed, tidied his desk and folded his clothing properly in his locker. He ensured that his boots were clean and highly polished.

The other soldiers prepared their rooms, too.

They all worked very hard, except for Pte Jenkins.

He watched television.

Sgt Wilson: 'Pte Jenkins!'
Pte Jenkins: 'Yes, sarge?'
Sgt Wilson: 'I want a word with you. I've just been with the Company Commander to inspect your room.'
Pte Jenkins: 'Oh, ... er . . . . . . yes, sarge?'
Sgt Wilson: 'You didn't sweep the floor or empty the waste bin . . . .'
Pte Jenkins: 'No, sarge.'
Sgt Wilson: 'You didn't prepare the room at all, did you?'
Pte Jenkins: 'No, sarge. You see, I didn't know about the inspection.'
Sgt Wilson: 'You didn't know? But it appeared on Company Daily Detail, and it's your responsibility to read all written orders. It's not good enough, is it?'
Pte Jenkins: 'No, sarge.'
Sgt Wilson: 'Right, stand by your bed at 1830 hours tonight for another inspection.'
Pte Jenkins: 'Yes, sarge.'
Sgt Wilson: 'And make sure you prepare the room properly or you'll be in serious trouble.'

B COMPREHENSION

Exercise 11:1

1. Why did Pte Thomas work hard in his room?
2. What did he do to the waste bin?
3. Where did he put his clothing?
4. What did he do to his boots?
5. What did Pte Jenkins do?
6. What excuse does Pte Jenkins give for not preparing his room?
7. Why is it not a good excuse?
8. When will Pte Jenkins have another room inspection?

C GRAMMAR FOCUS

Did you prepare your room?
He did not straighten out the mat.

Exercise 11:2
Look at the models:
Did you clean the room?
Did you clean behind the desk?
Now look at the table below, and practise asking similar questions:

<table>
<tr><td rowspan="2">Did you</td><td>clean
tidy</td><td>the room?
the desk?
the shelves?
the locker?
the wash area?</td></tr>
<tr><td>sweep
polish</td><td>the floor?
the mirror?
your boots?</td></tr>
</table>

Did you do it properly?

Did you	clean sweep wash	behind under inside	the desk? the bed? the sink?

Exercise 11:3

Pte Jenkins did not prepare his room for the inspection.
Look at the models:
He did not straighten out the mat.
He didn't straighten out the mat.

Now look at the picture and make similar sentences.

Exercise 11:4

1. After a football match, Pte Graham was in a hurry. He did not have a shower. He changed straight out of his sports kit into his uniform.
2. Before he went to bed, Pte Baker threw his trousers on the floor. He did nothing to them before he put them on again the next day.
3. Pte Martin left his map, a protractor and a valuable compass on the back of a vehicle after a map reading exercise.
4. The training period started at 0800 hours and Pte Sutton arrived at 0806 hours.
5. Capt Field was approaching the HQ building just as Pte Brown was leaving it. Pte Brown walked straight past Capt Field and ignored him.

Which soldier. . . . . .

1. . . . . . . did not look after his equipment?
2. . . . . . . did not salute an officer?
3. . . . . . . did not arrive on time?
4. . . . . . . did not keep his uniform tidy?
5. . . . . . . did not keep himself clean?

D VOCABULARY

Reference List

daily detail	locker	shelf (shelves)
desk	mat	sink
excuse	officer commanding (OC)	to stand by (your) bed
to ignore	responsibility	toiletry items
to inspect	to salute	wash area
inspection		waste bin

Exercise 11:5
Use words from the Reference List to complete the following sentences.

1. It is every soldier's ________ to read orders.
2. The order for the OC's ________ was on ________ ________.
3. He had no ________ for not preparing his room.
4. When a soldier passes an officer he must not ________ him.
5. When he is in uniform, a soldier must always ________ an officer.
6. During a room inspection, the soldiers have to ________ ________ their ________.

Exercise 11:6
This room is ready for inspection. Use words from the Reference List to name the numbered items.

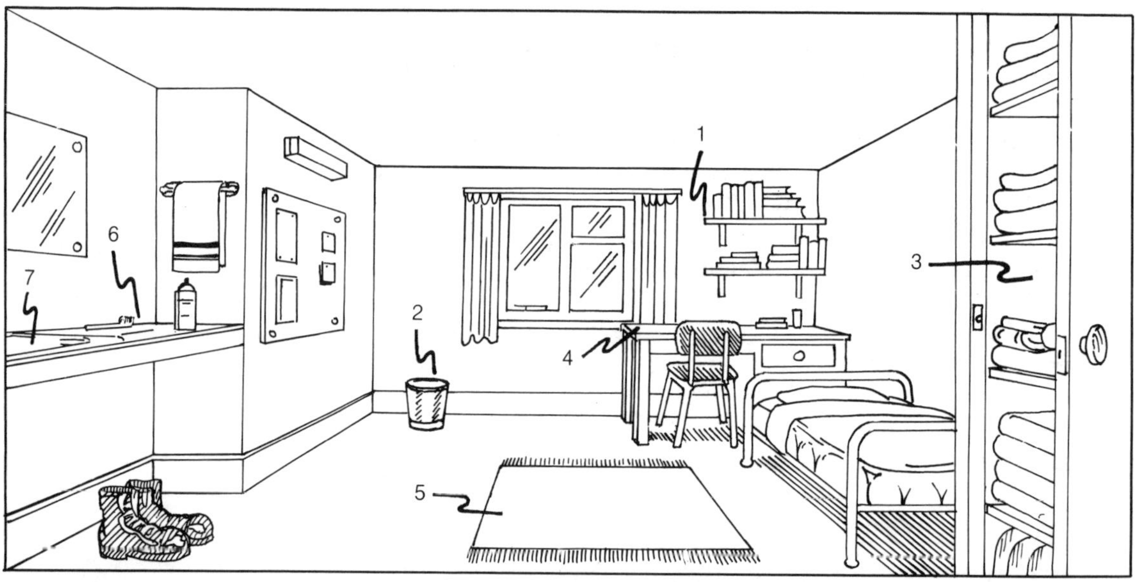

E DISCUSSION

Exercise 11:7

This unit is about a room inspection. How many other kinds of inspection can you think of? Do you think that there are good reasons for doing these inspections or do you think that they are a waste of time?

UNIT 12

BRIEFINGS

A | PRESENTATION

The OC of 'A' Coy is briefing his platoon commanders . . . . . .

'When we were in the field recently some of the soldiers couldn't use their compasses properly. This meant that some of the sections arrived late at their rendezvous.

This is not good enough.

You are to arrange a 24-hour exercise for your platoons as soon as possible. The purpose of the exercise will be to give your men practice in marching by day and by night across country using their compasses. I'll leave the details up to you.'

Now the platoon commander of No 3 Platoon is briefing his section commanders . . . . . .

'Pay attention and take notes.

The Company Commander is not happy with the standard of map reading. So, next Tuesday, 26th October, the whole platoon is going out on a 24-hour exercise, Exercise "Hot Foot".

The aim of the exercise is to give the platoon practice in compass marching across country. You will move by day and night.

The dress for the exercise will be fighting order. Weapons and ammunition will not be carried.

You are to draw combat rations for your sections from the stores. Do this at 1600 hours on Monday 25th October. Individuals will be responsible for their own meals during the exercise.

Each man is to take a protractor, a compass, Map Sheet 175, map-case, torch and chinagraph pencils. You are responsible for checking this.

The platoon is to parade outside the guardroom at 0730 hours on Tuesday 26th October. We shall travel to the exercise area by 4-tonner but we shall march back to camp.

Estimated time of return to camp will be 1030 hours on Wednesday 27th October. Make sure you brief your sections. Right, that's all. Any questions? . . . . . .'

Compass marching

B COMPREHENSION

Exercise 12:1

1. Why did some of the sections arrive late at their RVs?
2. What does the Company Commander think of the standard of map reading?
3. On which day does No 3 Platoon's exercise take place?
4. What is the purpose of the exercise?
5. What will the dress be for the exercise?
6. Will weapons and ammunition be carried?
7. At what time are section commanders to draw combat rations from the stores?
8. Where is the platoon to parade?
9. How will the platoon go to the exercise area?
10. How will they return to camp?
11. When is the estimated time of return to camp?

C GRAMMAR FOCUS

You will move by day and night.
You are to draw combat rations from the stores.
Dress will be fighting order.

Exercise 12:2
Look at the model:

You will practise compass marching.
You are to practise compass marching.
Dress will be fighting order.

Now make similar sentences from the tables below:

You	will are to	practise move wear be responsible for	compass marching. by day and by night. fighting order. cooking your own meals.

I	will am to	be responsible for collecting the rations.
You	will not are not to	carry weapons or ammunition.

Dress Equipment Transport Estimated time of return	will be	fighting order. protractor, compass, etc. for each man. by 4-tonner. 1030 hours, Wednesday 27 October.

Exercise 12:3
Cover the sentences in Exercise 12:2. Read the notes opposite taken during the platoon commander's briefing. Practise giving the briefing yourself.

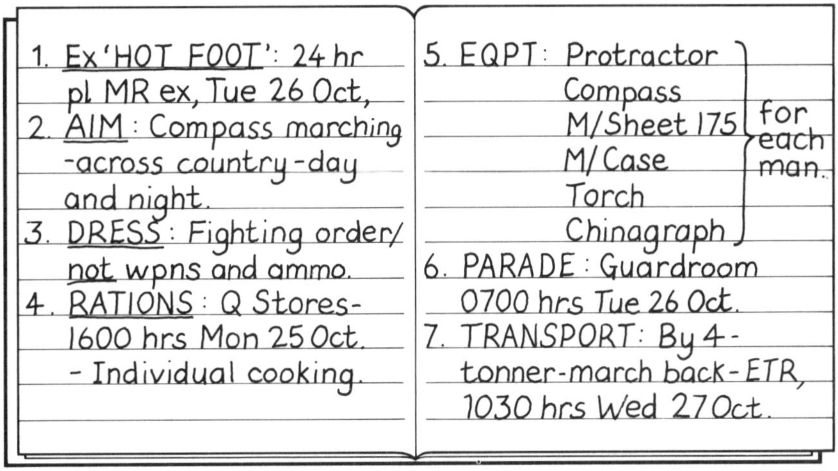

D VOCABULARY

Reference List

across country	estimated (time of departure/arrival/ return)	rendezvous
aim	map case	to be responsible for
to brief	map reading	to take notes
briefing	map sheet No	4-tonner
chinagraph pencil	protractor	torch
compass		

Exercise 12:4

Use words from the Reference List to complete the following sentences.

1. They can't use the roads. They must travel ________ ________.
2. In order to find their way and locate positions, all soldiers have to be good at ________ ________.
3. All platoon commanders are to attend the OC's ________.
4. The ________ for the platoon is the small wood south of Brookers Farm. We will meet there at 0035 hours.
5. The ________ of the exercise is to improve your skill in moving at night.
6. If you do not ________ ________ you might forget important details.
7. The platoon commanders ________ ________ ________ working out the details of the exercise.
8. Make sure you use the correct map. Check the ________ ________ ________.
9. These are not the exact timings. They are only ________.

Exercise 12:5
Use words from the Reference List to name the following.

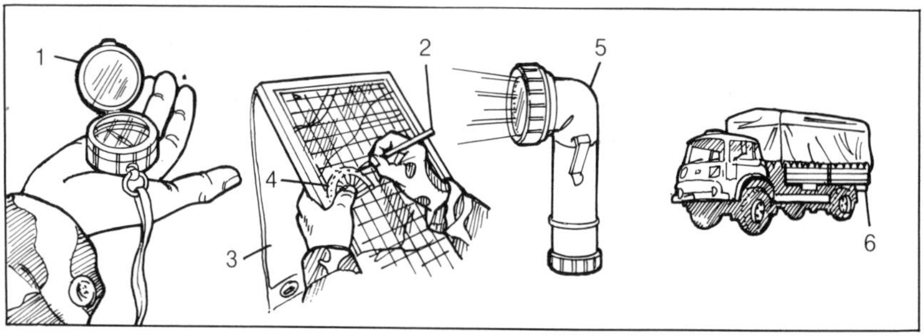

Exercise 12:6
Below are some military abbreviations you will often see. Find the full words in the Reference List.
1. RV 2. ETR 3. ETD 4. ETA

E DISCUSSION

Exercise 12:7
Can you think of a good way to begin and to end a briefing? What should you take with you to a briefing? Look at the platoon commander's briefing again. Here are the first three headings *Exercise Date and Name, Aim, Dress* – what other headings would you use for the rest of the briefing?

UNIT 13

PRISONERS OF WAR

A PRESENTATION

Sometimes in battle the enemy will give himself up to you rather than die. You must not kill an enemy soldier who is trying to surrender. You have to take him prisoner, and he becomes a prisoner of war. There are certain rules about the treatment of prisoners of war which you must follow.

A prisoner of war must give you the following information:

His name
rank
army number
and date of birth.

He does not have to give you any other information about his unit, its position, strength, weapons and so on.

You must not torture him or ill-treat him in any way to force him to give you this kind of information.

You have to search a prisoner of war. You must take from him anything which will help military intelligence, such as:

maps, notebooks, plans, orders, codes, etc.

You also have to take from him anything which might help him to escape, such as a knife, compass or torch.

He does not have to give you any personal property – family photographs, letters, rings, watches and so on.

If he is wounded or sick you have to make sure that he gets medical treatment as soon as possible. You also have to give him sufficient food, shelter and rest, but you may get him to do work.

B COMPREHENSION

Exercise 13:1

1. If an enemy soldier wants to surrender, what must you do?
2. What information must he give you?
3. What information does he not have to give you?
4. May you ill-treat a prisoner to obtain information?
5. Why do you have to take plans, orders, codes and so on from a prisoner?
6. Why do you have to take things like a knife, compass or torch from him?
7. Which items may a prisoner keep?
8. What must you do if he is wounded or sick?
9. What else must you do for him?

C GRAMMAR FOCUS

You must (*or* You have to) follow the rules.
You must not ill-treat him.
He does not have to give you certain information.
You may search him.

Exercise 13:2
Look at the pictures below. For each picture give the rule for treatment of prisoners of war.

You must not . . . . . .

He must give you . . . . . .

He doesn't have to give you . . . . . .

You must not . . . . . .

You must . . . . . .

You must take . . . . . .

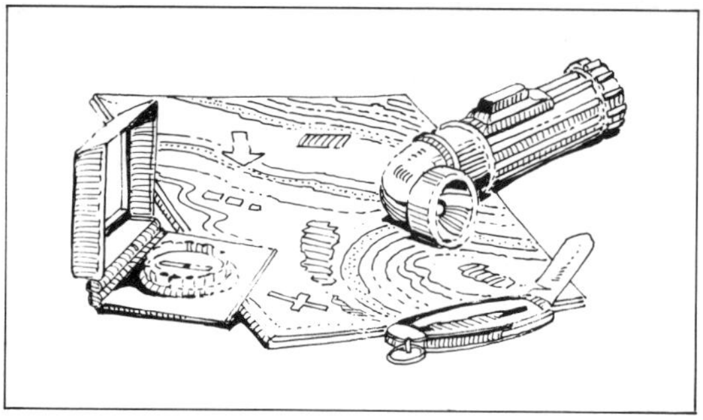

You must also take . . . . . .

He doesn't have to give you . . . . . .

You must . . . . . .

You may get him to . . . . . .

Exercise 13:3
Complete these sentences using the following words or phrases:

must must not do(es) not have to

1. A sentry ________ know how to raise the alarm.
2. A soldier must not load his weapon if he ________.
3. He ________ stay close to his weapon.
4. He ________ point his rifle in a safe direction.
5. You ________ light a fire, because the smoke could give your position away to the enemy.
6. You ________ walk to the exercise area, but you can if you like.
7. A soldier ________ train to improve his fitness.
8. When a soldier passes an officer he ________ ignore him.
9. On Saturday morning the men are free to rest. They ________do any work.
10. You ________ forget to collect the combat rations from the stores.

D VOCABULARY

Reference List

code	to ill-treat	roll call	tunnel
disguise	military intelligence	searchlight	watchtower
to escape	personal property	to surrender	wire cutters
false papers	prisoner of war	to torture	

Exercise 13:4
Use words from the Reference List to complete the following sentences.

1. ________ ________ is the part of the army which collects information about the enemy.
2. It is forbidden to ________ or ________ enemy prisoners in order to obtain information.
3. Letters, family photographs, watches, rings and so on are a prisoner's ________ ________.
4. Secret messages are usually sent in ________.
5. If a soldier is taken prisoner, it is his duty to try to ________.
6. When the enemy can fight no longer he will ________.
7. The abbreviation for ________ ________ ________ is PW.
8. During the escape, the prisoner of war wore a________ and carried ________ ________.
9. The prisoners have to answer their names at ________ ________.

Exercise 13:5
Use words from the Reference List to name the following.

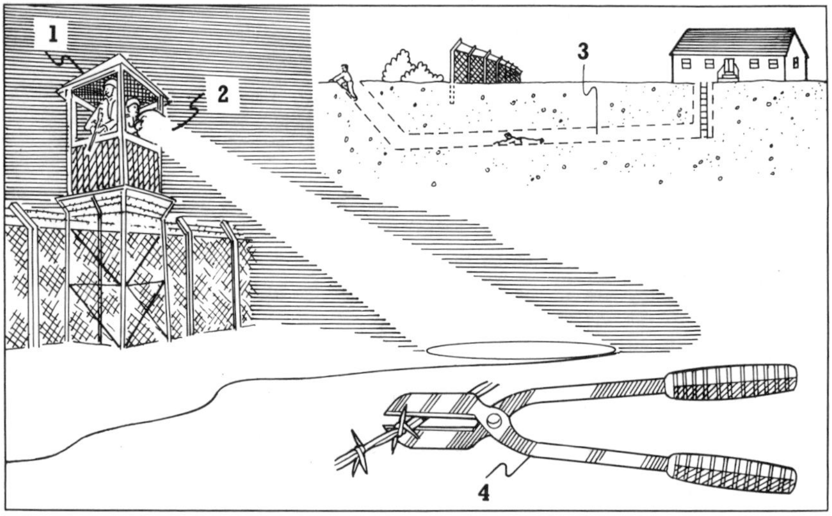

E DISCUSSION

Exercise 13:6
It is the duty of every soldier to try to escape if he is taken prisoner of war. What methods of escape from a prisoner of war camp do you know? (These words might help you: disguise – tunnel – false papers – wire cutters.) How can you prevent escapes? (These words might help you: roll call – watchtower – searchlight – dogs – barbed wire.)

UNIT 14

AN ARMY CAREER

A PRESENTATION

Lt Edwards is 28 years old. He applied to join the army 10 years ago. After a medical examination and a number of other tests he was accepted as a private soldier in an infantry regiment.

He completed his basic training which lasted 14 weeks.

His first posting was to a battalion in an infantry brigade. He served abroad for 3 years. Because he worked hard he was promoted to corporal. He commanded a section.

Cpl – Sect Comd

During the next few years he attended various courses, including a support weapons course and a mountaineering course.

He was selected early in his career as a potential officer, and he attended the officers training course at the military academy. This lasted for 6 months.

At the end of this time he was commissioned as a second lieutenant in his regiment.

Commissioned – 2Lt

He became a platoon commander and 2 years later he was promoted to lieutenant. He is studying for his promotion exams and he hopes to be promoted to captain in 4 years' time.

He got married the year before last. He lives in married quarters with his wife and young son.

Pl Comd – Lt

He enjoys playing football and he is interested in photography and mountaineering.

Interests and Hobbies

B COMPREHENSION

Exercise 14:1

1. How old is Lt Edwards?
2. When did he apply to join the army?
3. How long did his basic training last?
4. What sort of brigade was he posted to?
5. Where did he attend his officer training course?
6. How long did this last?
7. After he was commissioned what was his rank?
8. What was his appointment?
9. What is he studying for?
10. How many children has he got?
11. Where does he live?
12. What does he do in his spare time?

C GRAMMAR FOCUS

He joined the army ten years ago.
He has been in the army for ten years.

Exercise 14:2
Look at the model:
Question 1: When did he join the army?
Answer 1: He joined the army ten years ago.
Question 2: How long has he been in the army?
Answer 2: He has (He's) been in the army for ten years.

Now practise asking and answering questions about:
2Lt Fletcher
Staff Sergeant Cooke
Cpl Shepherd

Their biographies are below.

Exercise 14:3
Look at this table of biographies.

Name	**Martin Fletcher**	**Simon Cooke**	**Brian Shepherd**
Length of service	2 years	15 years	6 years
Age	23	33	24
Rank	2Lt	Ssgt	Cpl
Arm of service	Artillery	Engineers	Signals
Job before joining	University student	Toolmaker	Electrician
Training Courses	Officer training	Bridge building Demolitions	Radio telegraphist
Present job	Gun troop commander	Instructor, combat engineering	Communications centre
Hobbies	Skiing Music	Orienteering Birdwatching	Computer games

Ask and answer further questions about each man:

name	arm (Which arm does he belong to?)
age	former job (What was his job before he joined the army?)
rank	training courses (Which courses has he taken?)
present job	hobbies

Now, with a comrade, practise asking and answering questions about your own careers.

D VOCABULARY

Reference List

arm of service	demolitions	to promote (to be promoted)
artillery	engineers	promotion
basic training	gun troop	radio telegraphist
birdwatching	married quarters	regiment
to commission (to be commissioned)	military academy	to serve in the ranks
communications centre	mountaineering	signals
compulsory	orienteering	skiing
	photography	staff sergeant
	potential officer	

Exercise 14:4

Choose words from the Reference List which match the meanings below.

1. You must do it. You have no choice. It is ________.
2. A place which deals with signals messages is a ________ ________.
3. A group of three artillery guns is a ________ ________.
4. When you receive a higher rank you are ________. You get a ________.
5. One rank above sergeant is ________ ________.
6. If you are not an officer in the army you are serving ________ ________ ________.
7. If you are ________ it means you become an officer.
8. Officers are trained at a ________ ________.
9. ________ ________ are houses for soldiers and their wives.
10. The destruction of bridges, roads, buildings, etc. with explosives is known as ________.
11. A ________ ________ is a signaller who is specially trained at sending and receiving signals messages.

12. A ________ is one or more battalions of infantry who wear the same cap badge.
13. The part of the army that you belong to is your ________ ________ ________.
14. The arm that fires big guns is the ________.
15. The ________ build bridges, lay mines, etc.
16. The ________ deal with communications.
17. The first training that a soldier does is his ________ ________.
18. A soldier who might make an officer is known as a ________ ________.

Exercise 14:5
In which hobbies/interests are the following pieces of equipment used?

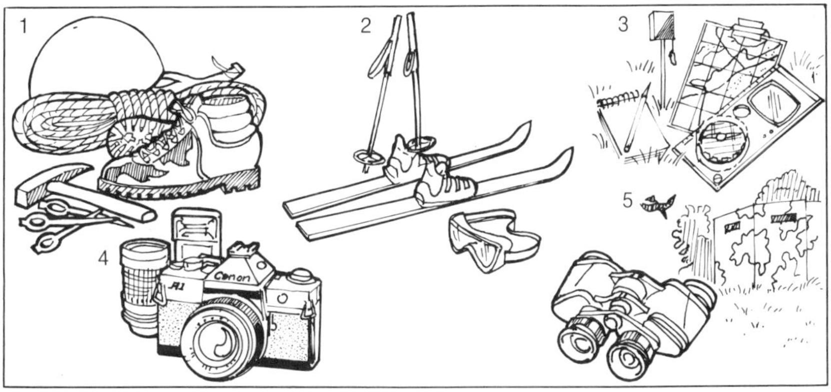

Exercise 14:6
Here are some military abbreviations that you will often see. Find the full words in the Reference List.

1. tp	4. regt	7. engr
2. arty	5. Ssgt	8. dml
3. MQ	6. sigs	9. COMMCEN

E DISCUSSION

Exercise 14:7
In the British Army most officers do not serve in the ranks before they are commissioned. How does this compare with your army? What do you think are the advantages and disadvantages of compulsory service in the ranks for all officers?

UNIT 15

PLATOON IN DEFENCE

A PRESENTATION

In the early hours of the morning the OC told No 1 Platoon Commander to hold the feature, nickname NEW PIN, against the enemy.

Since then Lt Smith has made a careful recce of the area in order to plan his defence. He has looked at the ground from the enemy's point of view.

He has decided on the likely enemy approaches. He knows from experience that enemy infantry like to use well-covered approaches close to the objective. Tanks are more likely to attack across open ground.

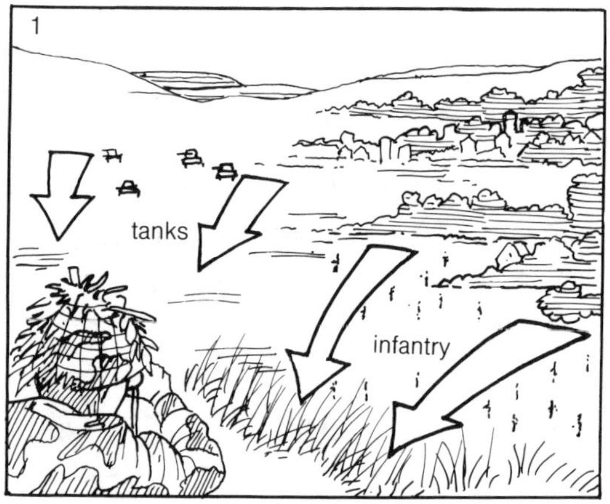

Likely approaches

He has placed the sections to give defence in depth, and sited platoon headquarters in a place which gives him the best control and communications.

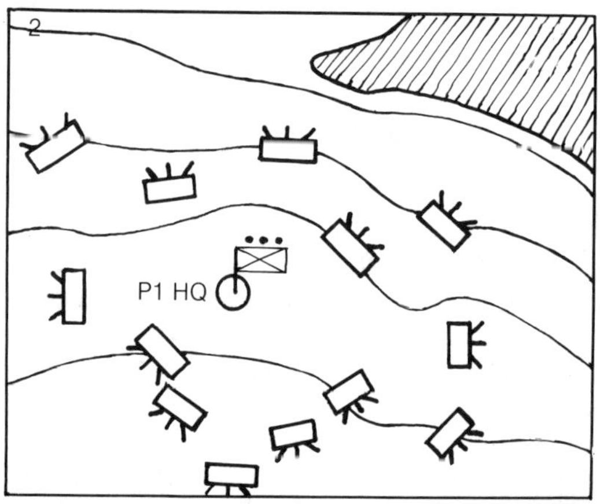

Defence in depth

He has sited platoon weapons as follows:
The anti-tank weapon to cover likely tank approaches. The three section machine guns where they will give the most effective fire against attacking enemy infantry. The mortar where it will give the most effective supporting fire.

Site anti-tank gun, machine guns and mortar

The sections have placed concealed obstacles such as wire, trip-flares and anti-personnel mines on likely enemy approaches to slow down an enemy attack.

Wire, trip-flares and mines

The section commanders have shown each man his post and arc of fire to ensure all-round defence.

Posts and arcs of fire

The men have dug in and have camouflaged their positions very carefully for the best safety and concealment.

Dig in and camouflage

The platoon commander is now going to send a radio message to his company commander. His defensive position is ready.

B COMPREHENSION

Exercise 15:1

1. What did the OC tell the commander of No 1 Platoon?
2. Why has Lt Smith made a careful recce of the ground?
3. What sort of approaches do enemy infantry like to use?
4. What sort of approaches are tanks likely to use?
5. Where has Lt Smith located platoon headquarters?
6. Which weapons will he use against attacking infantry?
7. What sort of concealed obstacles have the sections placed on the likely enemy approaches?
8. Why have the section commanders shown each man his post and arcs of fire?
9. What have the men done to ensure that they will be as safe as possible?
10. What is the platoon commander going to do now?

C GRAMMAR FOCUS

Lt Smith has made a careful recce.
The men have dug in.

Exercise 15:2
Look at the models:

1. He has made a careful recce.
2. He has looked at the ground from the enemy's point of view.

etc.

Now look at the platoon commander's check-list from his notebook. It shows the action he has taken.
Make statements about what he has done, following the models:

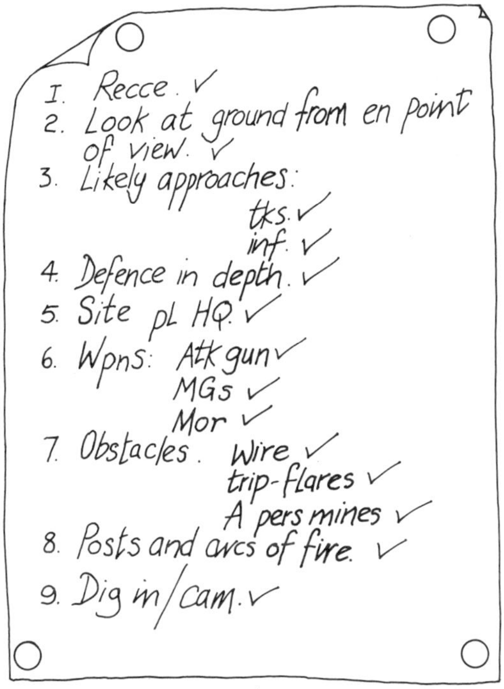

Have you briefed the platoon commander?

Exercise 15:3
Use the words to ask and answer questions.

Have Has	you they he	briefed the platoon commanders?

Yes	I have (I've) they have (they've) he has (he's)	done it already.

No	I have not (haven't) they have not (haven't) he has not (hasn't)	done it yet.

Words:
brief/platoon commanders.
collect/equipment.
prepare/rooms/inspection.
draw/stores/battle camp.
build/shelters.
report/operatons officer.
return/platoon headquarters.

D VOCABULARY

Reference List

all-round defence	to dig in	objective
anti-tank weapon	feature	obstacle
approach(es)	hasty defence	planned defence
arc of fire	mine (anti-personnel, etc.)	to site
to conceal	nickname	trip-flare
defence in depth		

Exercise 15:4
Use words from the Reference List to complete the following sentences.

1. When possible, soldiers must ________ ________ to give them protection in defence.
2. The hill was a ________ which the platoon commander could identify from the map.
3. The enemy wanted to capture NEW PIN. It was their ________.
4. On operations and exercises a ________ is often used for a feature instead of its real name.
5. The position was protected from attack from any direction. It had ________ ________ ________.
6. The sections were not placed in line. They were positioned so that they gave ________ ________ ________.
7. The ________ are the routes used by the enemy to get close to the objective.
8. Ditches, barbed wire and other ________ help to slow down an enemy attack.
9. The platoon was under attack. There was no time to lose and the platoon commander had to make a ________ ________.
10. When he ________ the mortar, the platoon commander chose a position where it would give the best supporting fire.

Exercise 15:5
Use words from the Reference List to name the following:

1

2

3
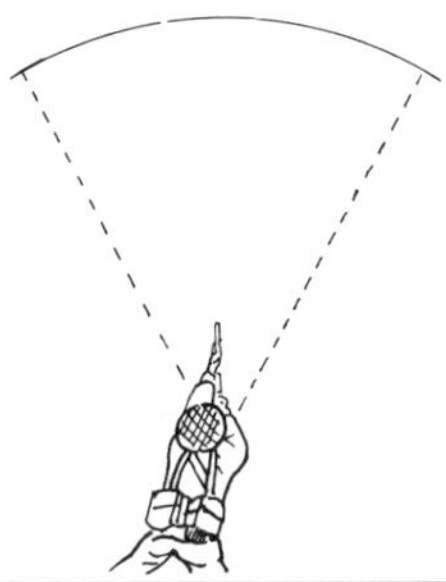

4

Exercise 15:6
Here are some military abbreviations that you will often see. Find the full words in the Reference List.
1. obj 2. obs 3. def 4. Apers 5. Atk

E DISCUSSION

Exercise 15:7
A famous general once said that defence must be active not passive. What do you think the terms 'active defence' and 'passive defence' mean? How can defence be made 'active'? Try to discover the meaning of 'hasty defence'. How does this differ from 'planned defence'?

UNIT 16

FIRE AND MANOEUVRE

A PRESENTATION

Sgt Ford is training some new recruits . . . . . .

1. The Role of the Infantry

'As infantrymen, this is what you have to do:

Capture and hold ground.

Close with the enemy and destroy him or force him to surrender.

You achieve this by fire and manoeuvre.

You must be able to operate by day and by night, in any weather and over any type of terrain.'

2. Fire and Manoeuvre

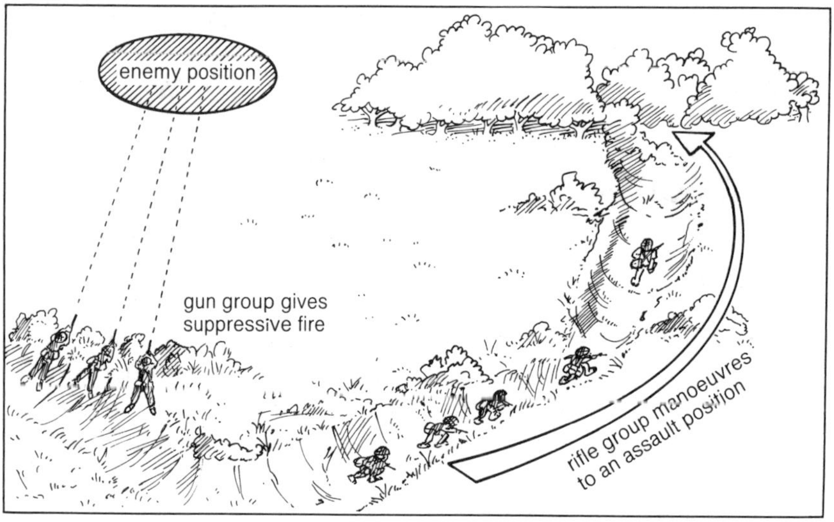

'The tactic you use to achieve your objective is called "fire and manoeuvre". Half of your force remains in position and fires at the enemy to keep his head down. In other words they give suppressive fire to protect the group that is moving. The group that is moving uses the natural features of the ground in a skilful way to get close to the enemy. In other words they manoeuvre into a good assault position.'

3. Individual Battle Drill

'If you come under fire, you must know what to do automatically – without thinking.

Drop to the ground and take cover.

Crawl to a new position, under cover if possible.

Observe: to locate the enemy's position.

Then return the enemy's fire.'

B COMPREHENSION

Exercise 16:1

1. When you find the enemy you must do one of two things. What are these two things?
2. Which basic principle of military tactics do you use to achieve your objective?
3. Under what conditions must you be able to operate?
4. What is the task of the group that remains in position?
5. What is their aim in doing this?
6. What is the aim of the group that is moving?
7. How do they use the natural features of the ground?
8. In what way must you perform the individual battle drill?
9. What is the first thing you do if you come under fire?
10. What two things do you do after you have moved to a new position?

C GRAMMAR FOCUS

This is what you have to do.
You must know what to do.

Exercise 16:2
Look at the model:
The section commanders don't know where the RV is.
The RV is in the wood.

Now fill in the statements below with 'what', 'when', 'where', 'who', 'why', or 'how', as appropriate. Then give the missing information by looking at the pictures.

1. The section commanders don't know ________ the RV is.

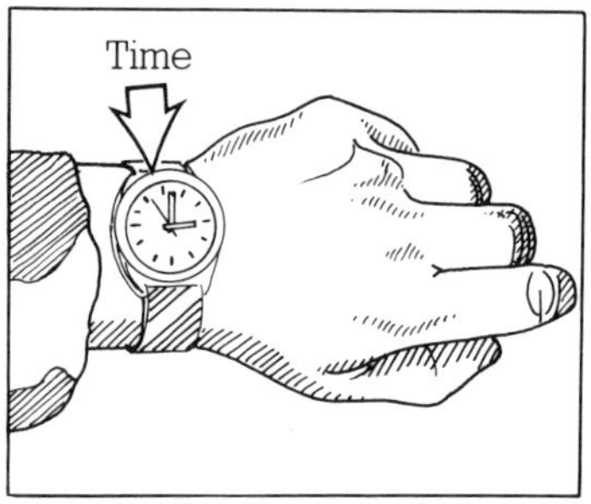

2. The section commanders don't know ________ they must arrive at the RV.

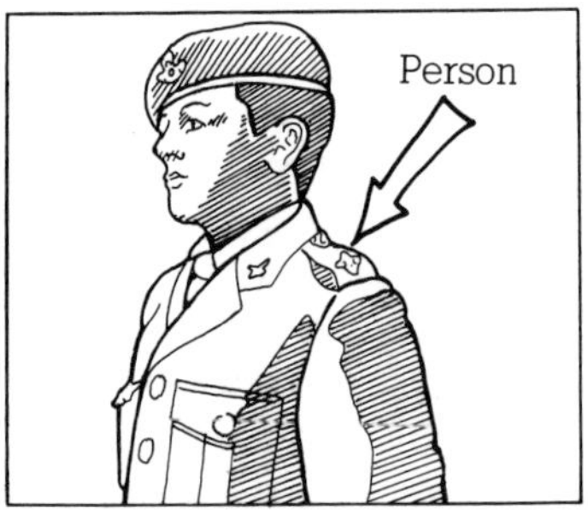

3. The corporal doesn't know ________ gave the order.

4. The recruits don't know ________ they will get to the exercise.

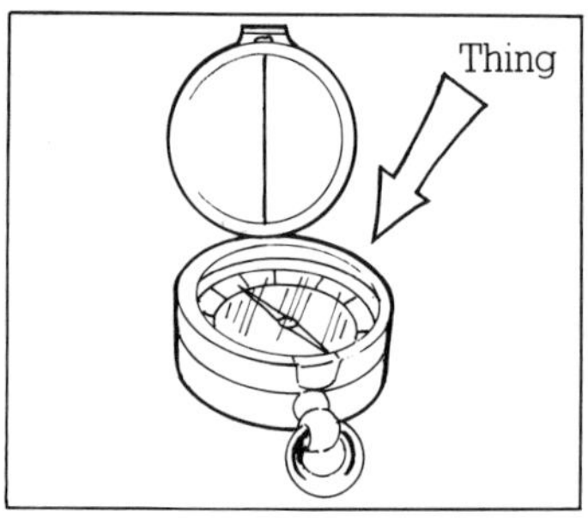

5. The recruits don't know ________ to bring on the exercise.

6. The OC wants to know ________ Pte Palmer is not here.

Exercise 16:3
Now complete the following sentences from the table and think of suitable responses yourself.

Please tell me	....	your name is. you live. your Commanding Officer is. you will be promoted. you travel from home to work. you are studying English.

Exercise 16:4
Look at the pictures below. Practise stating in full what the drill is if you come under fire.

Drop

Crawl

Observe

Return fire

D VOCABULARY

Reference List

assault	to drop down	to return fire
automatically	to force	skilful
to capture	force	suppressive fire
to close (with the enemy)	to hold (ground)	tactic
to destroy	to locate	to take cover
discipline	to manoeuvre	terrain
drill		

Exercise 16:5
Choose words from the Reference List which match the meanings below.

1. To get on the ground quickly ....
2. Fire which keeps the enemy's head down ....
3. To do something without thinking ....
4. A fighting unit ....
5. To take ground away from the enemy ....
6. To stop the enemy from taking your ground ....
7. Attack ....
8. To get where the enemy cannot see you ....
9. Another word for ground ....
10. A planned method of fighting ....
11. To find a position ....
12. To move making good use of the ground ....

Exercise 16:6
Use words from the Reference List to complete the following sentences.

1. When you come under fire you must ________ the enemy's fire as soon as possible.
2. When they move to an attack position the section made ________ use of the ground.
3. Soldiers must always obey orders so good ________ is necessary.
4. When soldiers know their ________ they can act without thinking.
5. If the enemy will not surrender, the infantry must ________ him.
6. The enemy will not give up easily so we must ________ him to surrender.
7. We must ________ with the enemy before we can attack him.

Exercise 16:7
Here are two military abbreviations you will often see. Find the full words in the Reference List.

1. tac 2. loc

E DISCUSSION

Exercise 16:8
What do you think the words 'drill' and 'discipline' mean?

Why are drills and discipline important to a soldier in battle?

UNIT 17

APPRECIATION

A	PRESENTATION

No 2 Section of No 3 Platoon have come under enemy small arms fire. The enemy appears to consist of four riflemen in a defensive position in front of an old farm building. The Section has taken cover in a ditch and returned fire.

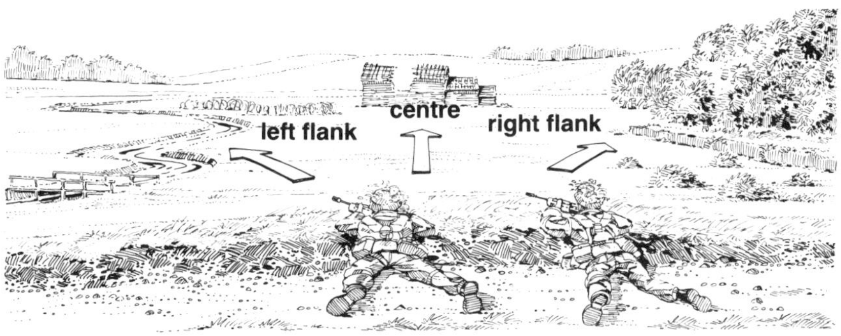

Cpl Scott, the Section Commander, has to decide what to do . . . . . .

'Shall I attack or withdraw? If I attack, shall I call for support? There are probably only four men in the enemy party. There are twice as many men in our section.

I am confident that I can defeat the enemy without calling for support. That is my aim.

How shall I divide the section? What will each group do?

I shall divide the section into two groups – the gun group (Nos 1 and 2 on the machine gun under command of the 2IC, Lance-corporal Turner) and the rifle group (myself and four riflemen).

Gun group task: they will give suppressive fire from this position in the ditch. Rifle group task: they will carry out the assault.

How shall I approach the enemy position? I have three choices.

Left: On the left flank there is a stream to cross and there isn't much cover. I think that the enemy have placed a wire obstacle out there.

Centre: This is open ground. There is no cover.

Right: On the right flank there is plenty of cover as far as the edge of the wood. But there is still a lot of open ground between the edge of the wood and the farm building . . . . . .'

B COMPREHENSION

Exercise 17:1

1. What has happened to No 2 Section?
2. Where is the enemy position?
3. What has the section done?
4. What is Cpl Scott's aim?
5. How many groups will he divide the section into?
6. There are 8 men in a section. How many men will there be in each group?
7. What is the task of the gun group?
8. What is the task of the rifle group?
9. What are the problems in approaching from the left flank?
10. Why will Cpl Scott not approach from the centre?
11. What is the problem in approaching from the right flank?

C GRAMMAR FOCUS

What do you plan to do?
What is your aim?
What will the gun group do?

Exercise 17:2

Imagine that this situation arose in a training exercise. The platoon commander wants to check Cpl Scott's plan of attack. On the next page are some questions he might ask.

<table>
<tr><td>What do you</td><td>aim
plan
intend</td><td colspan="3">to do?</td></tr>
<tr><td>What is your</td><td colspan="4">aim?
plan?
intention?</td></tr>
<tr><td rowspan="2">How many men</td><td>are there</td><td>in</td><td>the enemy
your</td><td>party?</td></tr>
<tr><td>will there be</td><td>in the</td><td>gun
rifle</td><td>group?</td></tr>
<tr><td>What will the</td><td>gun
rifle</td><td colspan="3">group do?</td></tr>
<tr><td>How</td><td>will you
do you plan to</td><td colspan="3">approach the enemy position?</td></tr>
</table>

Exercise 17:3
Pair Work

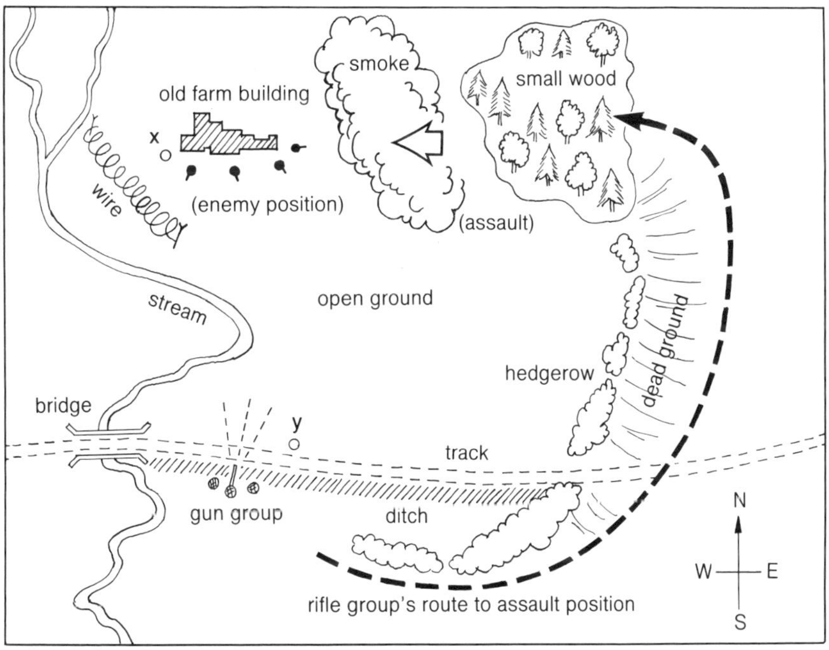

Go right flanking
Use hedgerow and dead ground as cover
Throw smoke grenades
Assault from edge of wood

Look at the sketch plan on the previous page.
Practise asking and answering questions – one student taking the part of the Platoon Commander, the other Cpl Scott.
For example:

Question 1: What is your aim?
Answer 1: My aim is to defeat the enemy.
Question 2: How many men are there in the enemy party?
Answer 2: There are probably only four.

D VOCABULARY

Reference List

appreciation	decision	to make an appreciation, a decision, plan, etc.
to attack	to defeat	
to call for support	ditch	orders
centre	to divide	plan
confident	flank	rifle group
cover	gun group	to withdraw
dead ground	lance-corporal (Lcpl)	wood
to decide		

Exercise 17:4
Use words from the Reference List to complete the following sentences.

1. When a commander thinks about the different ways of achieving his aim he makes an ________.
2. There may be more than one way of achieving his aim so he must ________ which one is the best.
3. When he has chosen the best way he can make his ________.
4. He can then give his ________ to his men.
5. For fire and manoeuvre, the corporal ________ his section into two groups.
6. The group with the machine gun for suppressive fire is called the ________ ________.
7. The group to carry out the assault is called the ________ ________.
8. If a commander needs help, he must ________ ________ ________.
9. The section commander was ________ that he could capture the enemy position so he decided to ________ it.
10. The platoon came up against an enemy company so they were forced to ________

Exercise 17:5
Use words from the Reference List to name the following.

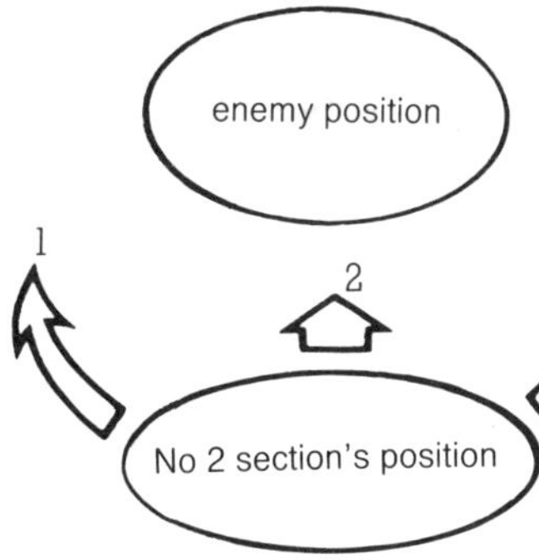

Exercise 17:6
Choose words from the Reference List which match the meanings below.

1. An area that cannot be observed by the enemy, though it might be in range of his weapons ....
2. To win a battle against the enemy, to beat him ....
3. Bushes, trees, hedges etc. in which a soldier can hide from the enemy ....

E DISCUSSION

Exercise 17:7
Imagine that you are the Section Commander of No 2 Section. Decide what you would do in this situation. When you have made your appreciation and decided on a plan, work out what orders to give to your men.

UNIT 18

SECTION IN THE ATTACK

A | PRESENTATION

The section has carried out the attack successfully. This is what happened.

The rifle group crawled along the ditch and then went behind the hedgerow. They made sure that they kept as low as possible. When they got into dead ground they were able to stand up and double. They entered the small wood from the east.

All this time the gun group laid down suppressive fire. They did this to keep the enemy's head down.

As soon as they were all in position, the rifle group formed up in extended line. The section commander threw a smoke grenade. This was the signal for the assault to go in.

The rifle group immediately charged forward towards the enemy. The gun group kept firing until the rifle group appeared through the smoke screen close to the enemy position.

The gun group stopped firing as the rifle group pressed the attack home. The enemy position was captured.

Immediately, the rifle group took up all-round defence. Now it was their turn to provide covering fire if necessary for the gun group.

The gun group manoeuvred forward to reorganise with the rest of the section.

B COMPREHENSION

Exercise 18:1

1. Where were the rifle group when they had to keep low?
2. When was it safe for them to stand up?
3. Why did the gun group lay down suppressive fire?
4. How did the rifle group form up when they were all in position?
5. What was the signal for the assault?
6. For how long did the gun group keep firing?
7. What did the rifle group do as soon as the enemy position was captured?
8. What would they do if the gun group came under enemy fire?
9. To complete the attack, what did the gun group do?

C GRAMMAR FOCUS

What did the rifle group do?
They crawled along the ditch.

When the section commander threw the smoke grenade, the rifle group charged forward.

When the rifle group captured the enemy position, they took up all-round defence.

Exercise 18:2
Look at the model:
What/rifle group/do?
What did the rifle group do?
They crawled along the ditch.

Now look at the pictures on the next page and ask and answer questions about the attack.

UNIT 18 SECTION IN THE ATTACK

What / rifle group / do?

1

Crawled

2

Moved

3

Entered

What / gun group / do?

4

Laid down

What / sect comd / do?

5

Threw

What / rifle group / do?

6

Charged forward

7

Captured

8

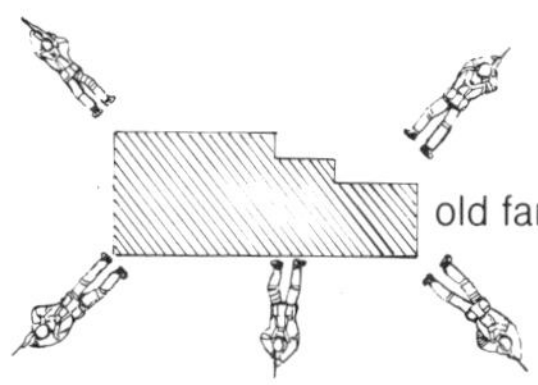

Took up

Exercise 18:3
Look at the model:
When the rifle group captured the enemy position, they took up all-round defence.

Now use the words to make sentences:

Words:
1. rifle group/capture/enemy position/take up/all-round defence.
2. gun group/see/rifle group/stop/firing.
3. soldiers/arrive/battle camp/draw/stores and equipment.
4. sentry/see/Lt Smith/challenge/him.
5. soldiers/march/range/fire/weapons.
6. Pte Allen/cut/hand/cover/injury/dressing.
7. platoon/capture/prisoner of war/search/him.
8. Maj Robinson/cross/stream/reach/operations tent.

D VOCABULARY

Reference List

arrowhead formation	double file	to press home an attack
to charge	extended line	to reorg (reorganise)
covering fire	to form up	signal
diamond formation	to keep low	single file
to double	to lay down fire	

Exercise 18:4
Use words from the Reference List to complete the following sentences.

1. The rifle group had to ________ ________ when they were moving in case the enemy saw them.
2. When the gun group moved, the rifle group were ready to protect them with ________ ________.
3. The gun group had to ________ ________ ________ on the enemy position for 10 minutes.
4. When the gun group saw the smoke grenade, they knew that this was the ________ for the assault to begin.
5. Before the section commander threw the smoke grenade he made sure his men were ________ ________ in the right positions for the assault.

Exercise 18:5
Choose words from the Reference List which match the meanings below.

1. To come together again after an attack ....
2. To move at twice the normal speed of marching ....
3. To run forward to attack the enemy ....
4. To finish an attack with speed and strength ....

Exercise 18:6
Name the diagrams of basic tactical formations shown below using words from the Reference List.

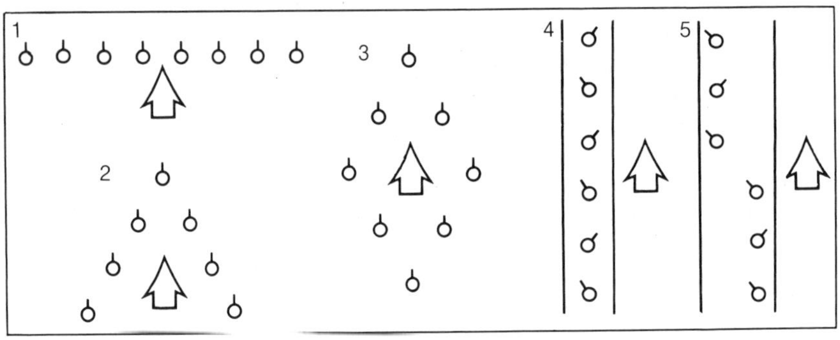

E DISCUSSION

Exercise 18:7
If you are planning to attack an enemy defensive position you will want as much information about him as you can get. What kinds of information about the enemy do you want? When extra help is needed in an attack, what kinds of support can a commander call for?

UNIT 19

DEBRIEFING

A PRESENTATION

The Section Commander, Cpl Scott, is speaking to his men about the exercise.

'On the whole you all did well.

Rifle group – most of you reacted quickly. You made good use of cover. You kept in formation during the assault. I was glad to see that you took up all-round defence automatically.

Gun group – you carried out your suppressive fire task effectively.

However, there are some points you will all have to improve on.

Before the exercise started you were told not to make a lot of noise in the approach. All of you made far too much noise in the wood.

Gun group – after we captured the enemy position you moved carelessly as you manoeuvred up to reorg with us. Pte Jenkins – I could see you easily. You moved across open ground when there was plenty of cover nearby. I know I told you to move quickly, but I also told you not to make yourself an easy target.

Some of you are still not fit enough. Pte Baker – at one point the muzzle of your rifle was almost digging into the mud. If you get dirt in your rifle it might not fire when you need it most.

Generally, the exercise was well done. But we can improve our fitness and individual battle skills and fieldcraft.'

B COMPREHENSION

Exercise 19:1

1. What is Cpl Scott speaking about?
2. How did the rifle group react?
3. Were they in the correct position as they assaulted?
4. After the assault, what formation did they take up?
5. What was wrong with the way they manoeuvred through the wood?
6. When did the gun group move carelessly?
7. What was wrong with the way Pte Jenkins manoeuvred?
8. What might happen if you get dirt in your rifle?
9. On the whole, did they carry out the exercise well or badly?
10. Which three areas can they improve on?

C GRAMMAR FOCUS

I told you to move quickly.
You were told not to make a lot of noise.

Exercise 19:2
Look at the model:
I told you not to make a lot of noise.
You were told to keep the muzzle out of the mud.
Now look at the pictures and make similar sentences:

1

Noise

2

Out of the mud

Fighting order

Light a fire

Take notes

Lock/in the desk

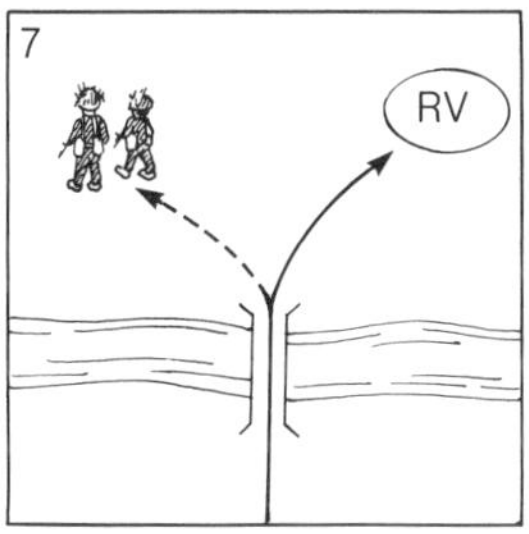

Turn right

Late

Exercise 19:3
Look at the model:
Lt Edwards told the runner to take a message.

Now use the words below to make similar sentences:

Words:
1. Lt Edwards / tell / runner / take / message.
2. Sentry / ask / officer / produce / identity.
3. Sgt Ford / remind / recruits / follow / safety / precautions.
4. Lt Edwards / encourage / Pte Jackson / run faster.
5. Lt Edwards / warn / Pte Allen / sterilise / water.
6. Sgt Wilson / order / Pte Jenkins / prepare / room inspection.
7. Capt Field / permit / men / rest / all day.
8. Maj Robinson / invite / Brigadier / watch / live-firing / demonstration.
9. The instructor / advise / recruits / wear / warm clothing.

Exercise 19:4

Look at the above words again. Who said . . . . . .?

1. 'Come on! You can catch him!'
2. 'Don't forget them!'
3. 'ID card please, sir.'
4. 'It's very cold today.'
5. 'Stand by your bed at 1830 hours!'

D VOCABULARY

Reference List

assembly area	forming up place	to react
axis of advance	forward edge of the battle area	start line
fieldcraft	H hour	target
final assault position	no-man's land	

The Reference List contains some important tactical terms that you have not met before.

Exercise 19:5

Choose words from the Reference List which match the meanings below.

1. Ground between our front line and the enemy ....
2. Thing you aim at when shooting ....
3. Line which marks the beginning of an attack ....
4. Time at which a unit crosses this line ....
5. What you do when you obey an order or when something happens to you ....
6. Camouflage, moving across ground and tactical formations are examples of this ....
7. Direction of a unit moving forward ....
8. Place where a unit gets into the correct positions ....
9. Area where units gather to rest, eat, check ammunition ....
10. The front line of our forces or the enemy's forces ....
11. Position where the last part of an attack goes in ....

Exercise 19:6
Look at the tactical diagram below and the abbreviations. Find the full words in the Reference List.

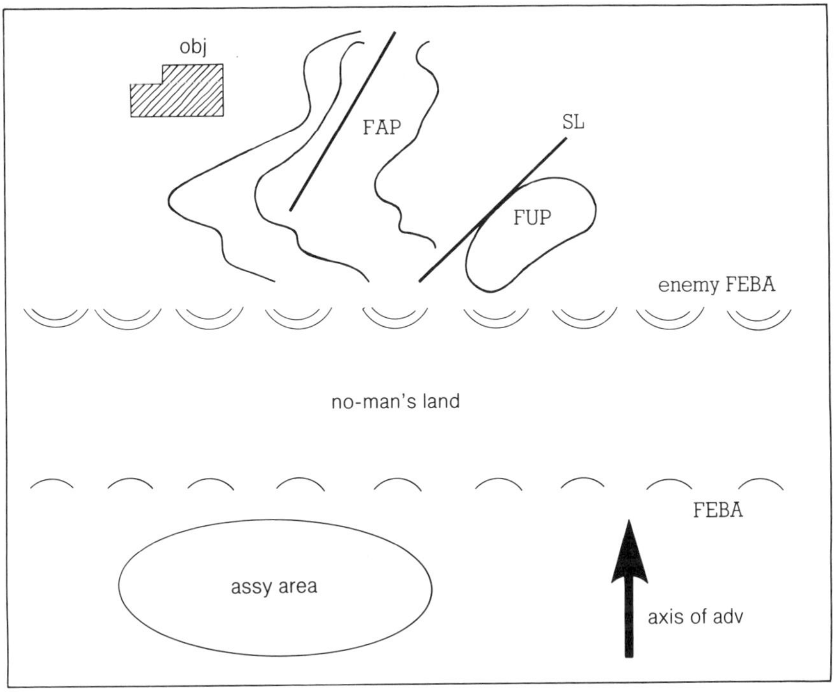

E DISCUSSION

Exercise 19:7
Cpl Scott's section carried out their attack exercise in terrain typical of Western Europe. Think about the differences between terrain and weather in your country and the types of terrain and weather in other countries. How might these differences affect the kinds of battle skill and tactic needed?

UNIT 20

ADVANCE TO CONTACT

A PRESENTATION

Lt Macdonald, the commander of No 1 Platoon of B Company, is reporting what happened during an advance to contact.

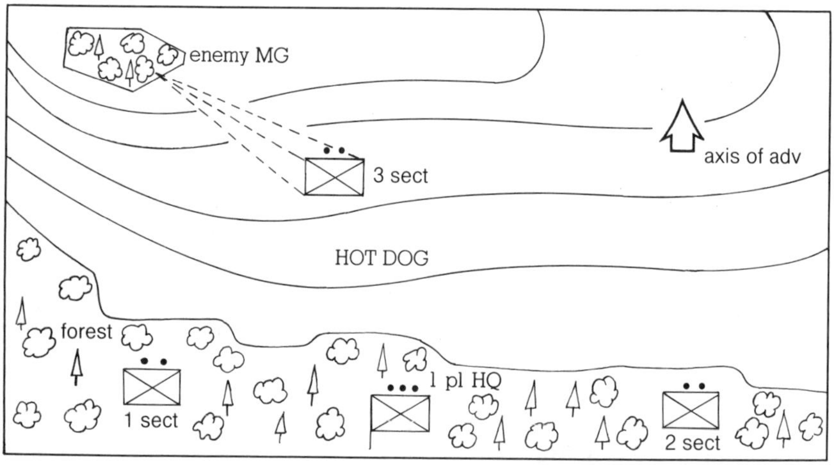

'My platoon was the point platoon. Our axis of advance was through the forest towards the ridge, nickname HOT DOG. No 3 Section was the leading section. Our orders were to destroy any pockets of resistance.

No 3 Section reached the crest of the ridge and took up all-round defence. Cpl Cooper, the section commander, made a quick appreciation of the ground to his front. He formed up his section into arrowhead formation and they moved forward.

The section were advancing down the forward slope of the ridge into open ground when they came under machine gun fire from the small group of trees on their left flank. Pte Richards was shot in the arm, but the wound was not serious.

The gun group immediately returned fire and Cpl Cooper threw a smoke grenade. While the gun group laid down suppressive fire, the rifle group withdrew to the dead ground on the reverse slope of the ridge under cover of the smoke screen. The rifle group then engaged the enemy so that the gun group could manoeuvre back to reorganise.

My radio operator sent a contact report to B Company commander. I moved Platoon HQ and Nos 1 and 2 Sections up to HOT DOG in support.'

B COMPREHENSION

Exercise 20:1

1. Where did the axis of advance lead to?
2. What were their orders?
3. What did Cpl Cooper do when No 3 Section reached the crest of the ridge.
4. Which formation were No 3 Section in when they moved forward?
5. Where did the machine gun fire come from?
6. What happened to Pte Richards?
7. What did the gun group do immediately?
8. What did Cpl Cooper do?
9. Where did the rifle group withdraw to?
10. Why did the rifle group engage the enemy?
11. What did the platoon radio operator do?
12. What did Lt Macdonald do?

C GRAMMAR FOCUS

The section were advancing down the forward slope when they came under machine gun fire.

Exercise 20:2

Look at the model:

Question 1: What happened to Pte Richards?
Answer 1: He was shot in the arm.
Question 2: How did it happen?
Answer 2: He was advancing down the forward slope when he came under machine gun fire.

Now look at the pictures and the words next to them. Ask and answer questions about each man.

UNIT 20 ADVANCE TO CONTACT

1. What/ happen/ Pte Richards?
   shoot/ arm.
   How/ happen?
   advance/ forward slope/ come under/ machine gun fire.

2. What/ Pte Simpson?
   broke/ toe.
   How/ happen?
   unload/ box/ fall/ foot.

3. What/ Pte Fowler?
   injure/ shoulder.
   How/ happen?
   train/ assault course/ slip/ fall/ ground.

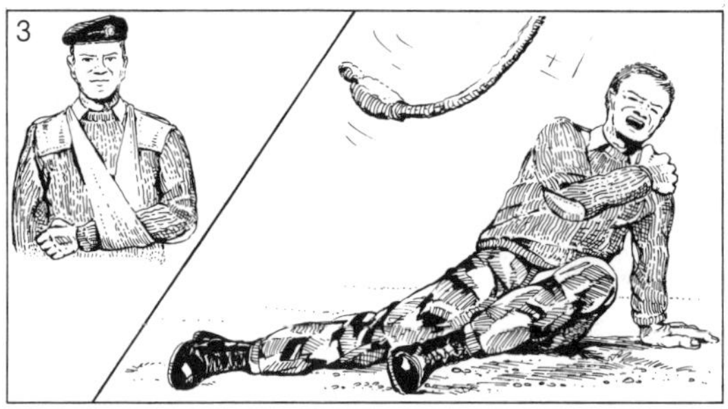

4. What/ Cpl Shepherd?
   break/ jaw.
   How/ happen?
   escort/ prisoner/ hit/ face.

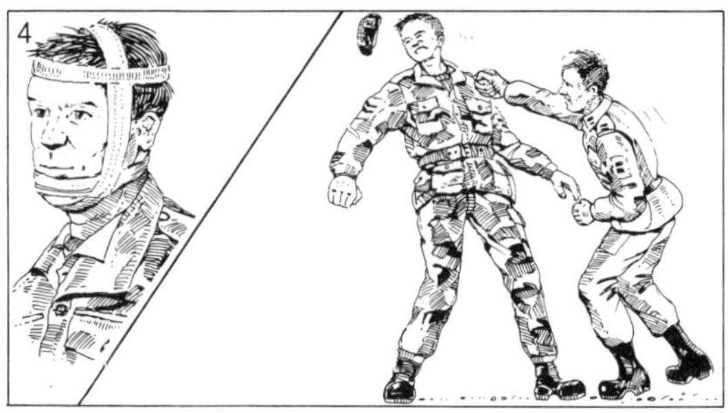

5. What/ Pte Green?
   hurt/ eye.
   How/ happen?
   travel/ back/ vehicle/ stone/ fly up.

D VOCABULARY

	Reference List	
to advance	to escort	reverse slope
advance to contact	forward slope	ridge
casualty	leading section	slope
contact report	orders group (O gp)	wound
crest	pocket of resistance	
to engage the enemy	point platoon	

Exercise 20:3
Use words from the Reference List to complete the following sentences.

1. The Company Commander will give his instructions to Platoon Commanders at his ________ ________ at 1530 hours.
2. As soon as you find the enemy you must send a ________ ________ to Company HQ.
3. The enemy has left behind ________ ________ ________ to delay our advance.
4. When you have contact you must ________ ________ ________ and call for support.

Exercise 20:4
Choose words from the Reference List which match the meanings below.

1. To move forward to get in touch with the enemy ....
2. To go with someone to protect or guard them ....
3. Any soldier who is killed, injured or sick ....
4. An injury in which the flesh is broken and blood flows ....

Exercise 20:5
Look at the diagrams below. Use words from the Reference List to complete the sentences.

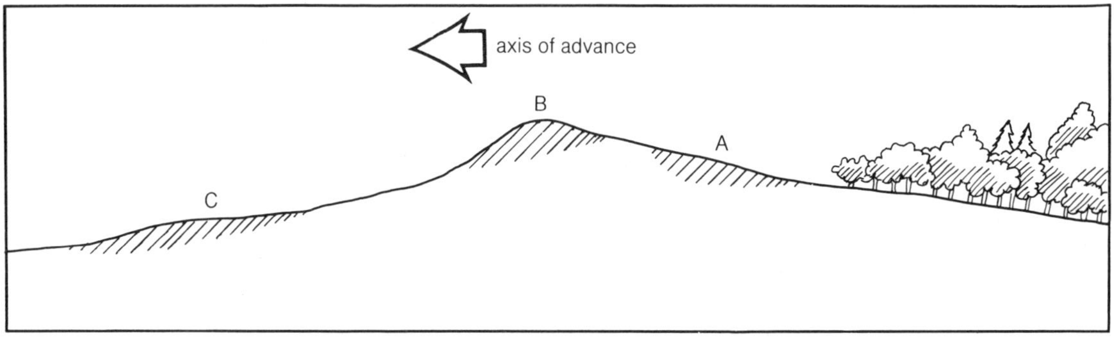

1. This feature is a ________.
2. Point 'A' is the ________ ________.
3. Point 'B' is the ________.
4. Point 'C' is the ________ ________.

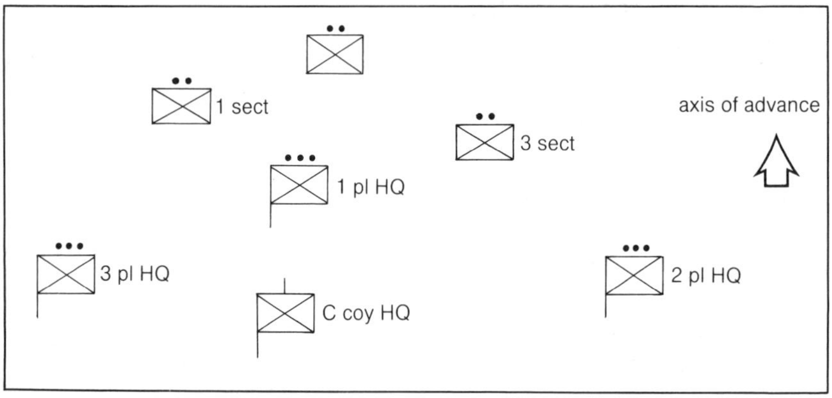

5. No ________ Section is the ________ ________.
6. No ________ Platoon is the ________ ________.

E DISCUSSION

Exercise 20:6
Imagine you are the commander of No 1 Platoon. You have just moved up to the ridge in support of your leading section. Make a quick appreciation and plan of attack. What orders will you give at your orders group to your section commanders? Remember that you have a casualty, Pte Richards.

PROGRESS TEST 3 (Units 11–15)

Read the following sentences and choose the best answer.

1. The soldier ________ read all written orders.
   a) has to b) may c) mustn't
2. He always ________ his boots.
   a) sweeps b) folds c) polishes
3. Pte Brown walked straight past the officer; he did not ________ him.
   a) look after b) salute c) inspect
4. The ________ points to north.
   a) compass b) protractor c) map
5. The men ________ outside the guardroom at 0800 hrs.
   a) paid attention b) practised c) paraded
6. Use a ________ to see the map at night.
   a) map case b) torch c) chinagraph pencil
7. The men left the camp at 0700 hrs and it will take them five hours to get to the exercise area, so their estimated time of ________ is 1200 hrs.
   a) arrival b) departure c) return
8. A soldier sometimes gives himself up rather than ________
   a) become a prisoner. b) surrender. c) get killed.
9. A PW ________ give you his name, rank and number.
   a) must b) must not c) does not have to
10. A PW camp usually has ________ to prevent an escape.
    a) wire cutters b) barbed wire c) tunnels
11. Lt Edwards joined the army ________
    a) during the next five years. b) in four years time.
    c) ten years ago.
12. He was ________ before he joined the army.
    a) commissioned b) promoted c) examined
13. Lt Smith has placed the sections to give defence ________
    a) in an OP. b) in depth. c) in the distance.
14. Because the pl comd must send messages, HQ is in a place which gives the best ________
    a) communications. b) concealment.
    c) camouflage.
15. Concealed objects have been placed to ________
    a) give all-round defence.
    b) allow effective supporting fire.
    c) slow down the enemy attack.

PROGRESS TEST 4 (Units 16–20)

Read the following sentences and choose the best answer.

1. The ________ Pte Parker is not here is that he broke his arm.
   a) means b) reason c) person
2. The sections don't know ________ they will get to the exercise.
   a) who b) what c) how
3. If you come under fire the first thing you do is ________
   a) drop. b) crawl. c) return fire.
4. When we close with the enemy we must destroy him or ________
   a) hold ground. b) remain in position. c) force him to surrender.
5. Fire at the enemy to ________
   a) remain in position. b) take cover. c) keep his head down.
6. There are only four men in the en party: there are ________ as many in our sect.
   a) just b) twice c) half
7. My aim is to ________
   a) attack or withdraw. b) defeat the en. c) divide the sect.
8. The gun group ________ suppressive fire.
   a) carried out b) formed up c) laid down
9. When the sect comd threw the smoke grenade the rifle group ________
   a) formed up in extended line. b) charged towards the en. c) took up all-round defence.
10. To move at about twice the speed of normal marching is to ________
    a) charge. b) reorganise. c) double.
11. They did it without thinking: in other words they did it ________
    a) quickly. b) effectively. c) automatically.
12. I told you to________ during the assault.
    a) keep in formation b) make yourself an easy target c) move across open ground
13. Lt Macdonald reported what happened during ________
    a) a pocket of resistance. b) an axis of advance. c) an advance to contact.
14. The leading section is called the ________ section.
    a) point b) orders c) arrowhead
15. When Pte Richards was shot the gun group ________ the enemy.
    a) engaged b) escorted c) laid down

VOCABULARY LIST

This list includes all words given in the Reference Lists in the units. The numbers after the words are unit numbers. Abbreviations are also listed with their full forms (eg ac = aircraft).

ac = aircraft
academy
  military academy 14
accurate 9
across country 12
active defence 15
activity, activities 2
to advance to contact 20
advance
  axis of advance 19
agile 8
agility 8
aim 12
aircraft (ac) 9
alarm
  to raise the alarm 4
all-round defence 15
  to take up all-round defence 18
to ambush 8
ambush drill 8
ammo = ammunition
ammunition (ammo) 1
  round of ammunition 1
anti-personnel mine (Apers mine) 15
anti-tank weapon (Atk) 15
APC = armoured personnel carrier
Apers mine = anti-personnel mine
to apply the safety catch 7
appointment 14
appreciation 17
  to make an appreciation 17
to approach 2, 4
approach, approaches 15
arc of fire 15
area
  assembly area 19
  battle area 19
  built-up area 6
  forward area 2
arm of service 14

VOCABULARY LIST

bottle
  water bottle 1
br = bridge
bridge (br) 2
to brief 5
briefing 6, 12
brigade (bde) 5
built-up area 6
butt 7

cal = calibre
calibre (cal) 9
to call for support 16
call
  roll call 13
to camouflage 2
camouflage net 1
camp 6
capt = captain
captain (capt) 4
to capture 16
card
  identity card 5
case
  map case 12
casualty 20
catch
  safety catch 7
centre 16
to challenge 4
to charge 18
charge
  in charge 7
charge
  explosive charge 2
check-list 15
chinagraph pencil 12
civilian 1
to clear 7
clear 7
to close with the enemy 16
code 13
combat jacket 1
combat kit 1
combat rations 1
combat trousers 1
COMMCEN = communications centre
comd = commander
to command 3
in command 3
commander (comd) 3
to commission, to be commissioned 14

VOCABULARY LIST

to keep in formation 19
to take up a formation 19
forward area 2
forward edge of the battle area (FEBA) 19
forward slope 20
front pouch 1
full kit 2

to give oneself up 13
grenade 1
smoke grenade 1
high explosive grenade 1
ground
to cover ground 8
dead ground 17
to hold ground 15, 16
open ground 5
group
gun group 17
orders group 20
rifle group 17
guardroom 12
gun
machine gun 1
sub-machine gun 3
gunner 9
gun group 17
gun troop 14
gymnasium (gym) 8

H hour 19
to halt 4
by hand 3
hasty defence 15
head
to keep one's head down 16
headquarters (HQ) 3
to heat 2
hedge 5
helmet
steel helmet 1
high explosive grenade 1
to hold a feature, ground, etc 15, 16
HQ = headquarters
hull 9

ID = identity
to identify 4
identity (ID) 5
identity card 5
to ignore 11
to ill-treat 13

posn = position
post 4
  information post 5
  observation post 2
posting 14
potential officer 14
pouch 1
  front pouch 1
  rear pouch 1
precautions
  normal safety precautions 7
to press home an attack 18
prisoner of war (PW) 13
private (pte) 3
to promote, to be promoted 14
promotion 14
property
  personal property 13
protection 9
protractor 11, 12
pte = private
ptl = patrol
PW = prisoner of war

quarters
  married quarters 14

rad = radio
rad op = radio operator
radio (rad) 3
radio operator (rad op) 3
radio telegraphist 14
to raise the alarm 4
range 6
rank (rk) 4
  commissioned rank 4
ranks
  to serve in the ranks 14
rations 1
  combat rations 1
to react 19
rear pouch 1
recce = reconnaissance
reconnaissance (recce) 2
recruit 16
regiment (regt) 14
regt = regiment
to release the safety catch 7
reliable 9
rendezvous (RV) 12
reorg = reorganise
to reorganise (reorg) 18
to report 5

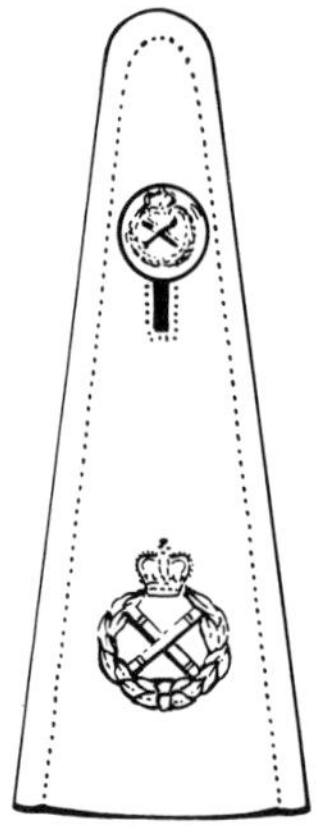

Field Marshal

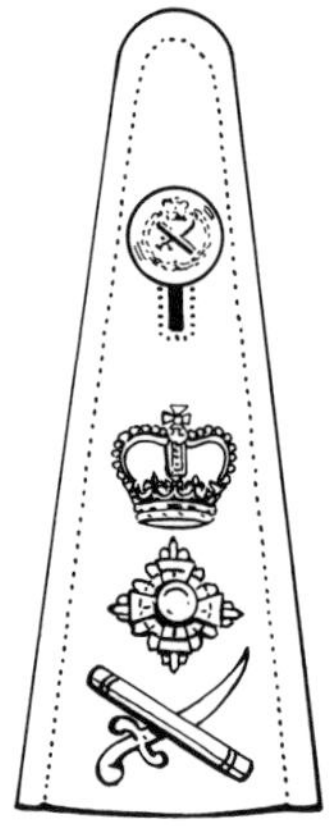

General

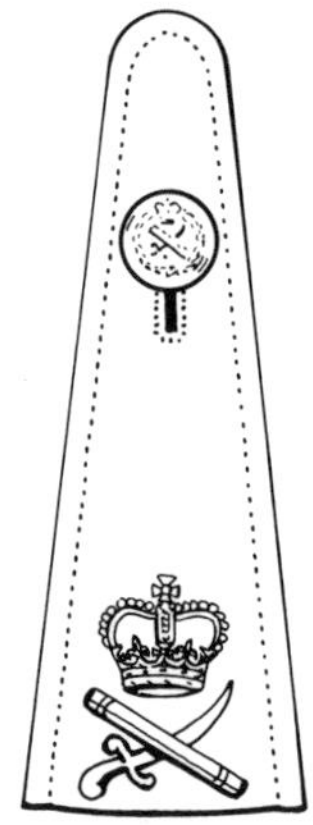

Lieutenant General

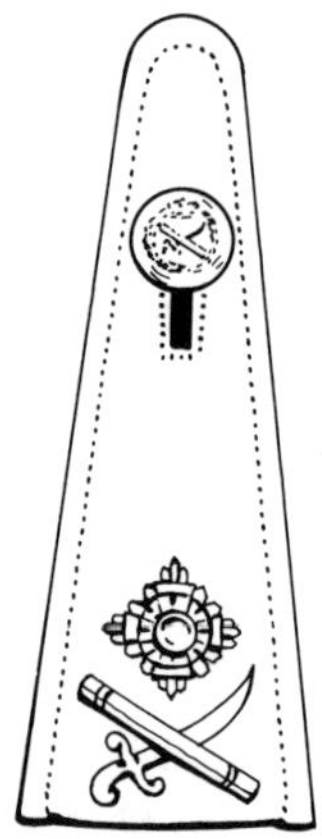

Major General

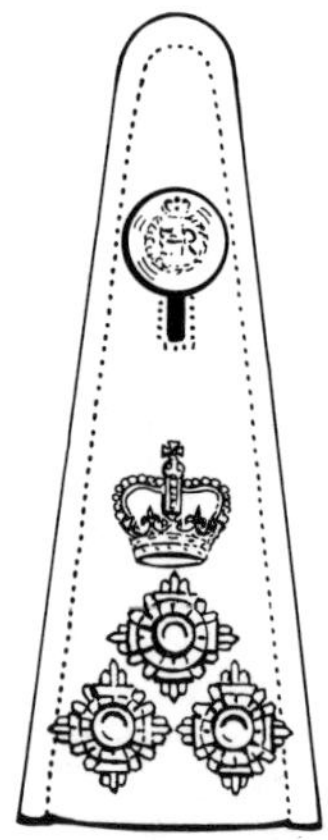

Brigadier

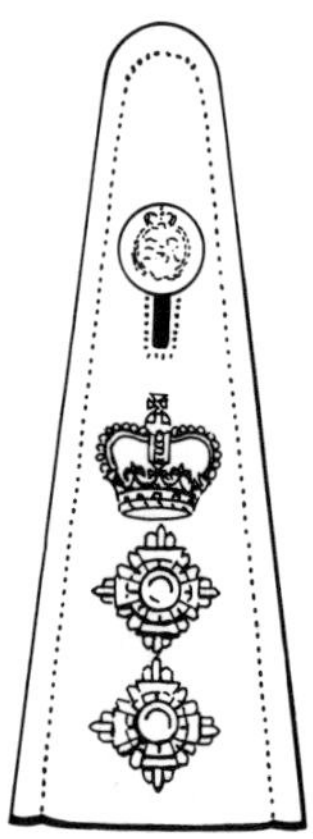

Colonel

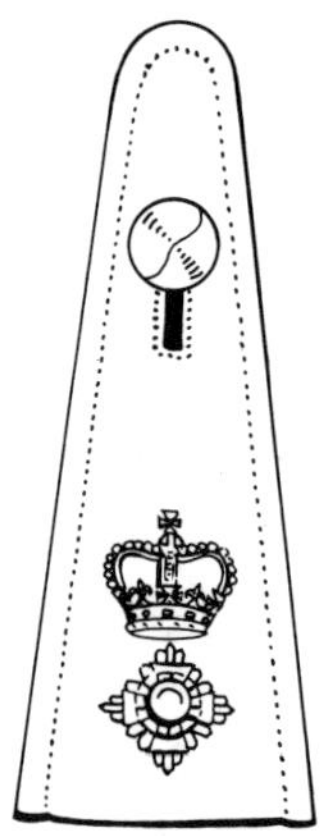

Lieutenant Colonel

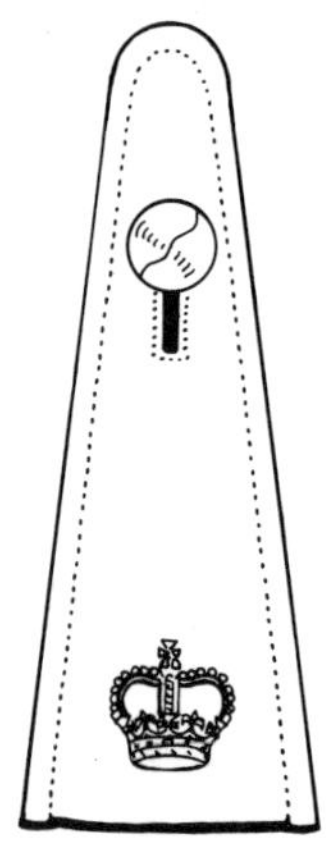

Major